THIS FLOWING TOWARD ME

This Flowing Toward Me: A Story of God Arriving in Strangers conveys with energetic wit and wisdom the surprising presence of God in the dailyness of life, with all its joys and sorrows, its fears and fancies, dreams and difficulties. The starting point is the author's unexpected insertion into the world of refugees. The endpoint is nothing less than graced union with the God for whom we all yearn. Treat yourself to this book: It will surely change the way you think about strangers and aliens—and quite possibly change your understanding of who God is and where God dwells and how you two could meet.

Peter van Breemen, S.J.
Author of *The God Who Won't Let Go*

A warm, personal, and inviting memoir about one of the most important issues of our time—the refugee crisis—told through the eyes of a remarkable woman of faith. In Sister Marilyn's beautiful new book, you will not only encounter a remarkable gathering of men and women, but also better understand how much the poor have to teach us about life, about hope, and about God.

James Martin, S.J.
Author of *This Our Exile: A Spiritual Journey With the Refugees of East Africa*

THIS FLOWING TOWARD ME

A STORY OF GOD ARRIVING IN STRANGERS

MARILYN LACEY, R.S.M.

ave maria press AMP notre dame, indiana

© 2009 by Marilyn Lacey, R.S.M.

All rights reserved. No part of this book may be used or reproduced in any manner whatsoever, except in the case of reprints in the context of reviews, without written permission from Ave Maria Press®, Inc., P.O. Box 428, Notre Dame, IN 46556.

Founded in 1865, Ave Maria Press is a ministry of the Indiana Province of Holy Cross.

www.avemariapress.com

ISBN-10 1-59471-197-6   ISBN-13 978-1-59471-197-8

Cover and text design by Brian C. Conley.

Cover image © Corbis Images.

Printed and bound in the United States of America.

Library of Congress Cataloging-in-Publication Data

Lacey, Marilyn.
   This flowing toward me: a story of God arriving in strangers / Marilyn Lacey.
      p. cm.
   Includes bibliographical references.
   ISBN-13: 978-1-59471-197-8 (pbk.)
   ISBN-10: 1-59471-197-6 (pbk.)
   1. Lacey, Marilyn. 2. Church work with refugees. 3. Spiritual life—Catholic Church I. Title.
   BX2347.8.R44L33 2009
   261.8'328--dc22
                              2008044396

To my parents, Ila and Ray, who gave me the
confidence to follow my heart's deepest desire.
And to the refugees, who are teaching me what
matters most: a whole new way of loving.

For sixty years I have been forgetful

Every minute, but not for a second

Has this flowing toward me stopped or slowed.

I deserve nothing. Today I recognize

That I am the guest the mystics talk about.

I play this living music for my Host.

Everything today is for the Host.

—from "The Music" by Rumi

CONTENTS

FOREWORD

The eminent twentieth-century Jewish philosopher and writer, Martin Buber, oddly declared that "success is not a name of God." His insight may be particularly difficult for us Americans to comprehend, much less embrace. We are, after all, a nation of achievers. We are heirs of the Puritan ethic of hard work and self-development. We measure our progress by resumé and recognition and social standing. We gauge our net worth by, well, net worth. The God who rewards effort and uprightness is the God most of us strive to worship.

The stories in this book, however, reveal a God altogether different from the kind of God we have fashioned in the West. This book describes a God aligned with the poor, a God whom we may meet when we open our doors to strangers and outcasts, when we choose to be among those for whom success is only a distant or shattered dream. These stories have the ring of authenticity, emerging as they do from the life experiences of the author, a Catholic nun who has spent the past quarter-century working with refugees and immigrants from Africa, South and Southeast Asia, Eastern Europe, and Latin America.

What I learned over time in my own relationships with condemned prisoners on death row, Marilyn Lacey has learned in dusty refugee camps and in seeing the struggles of displaced persons slowly piecing their lives back together. That learning is at once simple yet revolutionary: God is close to the broken-hearted. Life is about compassion, not perfection. We are all kin, and there are blessings galore for anyone willing to step beyond the fears that keep us apart. These stories are, therefore, filled with unmistakable joy even in the midst of suffering.

So go ahead. Delve into these pages. Discover for yourself how the author, with a lively mix of humor, insight, and compassion, invites those of us living behind locked doors in a world shuttered by homeland security to risk engaging unknown neighbors near and far, and there discover, perhaps to our unending surprise, that where we most felt threatened, a wealth of blessings instead awaits us.

Helen Prejean, C.S.J.
Author of *Dead Man Walking*

$\mathcal{P}$REFACE

According to an African proverb, a person who sees something good *must* tell the story. I have seen something good, and friends who know of my experiences with refugees have prodded me to write a book. For years I dismissed the idea, but the truth is that I am a happy person living what I feel is a fascinating life. Perhaps that's rare enough in our troubled world to justify this account of the source of my joy, found in the ordinariness of welcoming the strangers in our midst.

Looking over forty years of my life as a Catholic nun, the past twenty-five spent with refugees from some of this planet's most ravaged places, it's difficult to know where to begin. Authors more talented than I am have already written books about refugees, and I do not presume to add my name to those who expound on spirituality. My intent, rather, is to convey how those two seemingly separate worlds—on the one hand, the gritty, desperate, resilient lives of refugees who seem so different from us, and on the other, the startling, life-altering, graced immediacy of the God whose nearness we all secretly long for—have merged in my life. I invite the reader to step into my personal story, to glimpse in these pages what I have stumbled upon in the convergence of my spiritual life and my relationships with the refugees: namely, the challenging, consoling, bewildering, healing, and ever-surprising presence of a God who comes to us precisely where we least expect.

I begin with an image borrowed from Mechtild of Magdeburg, a thirteenth-century European woman. Let these words she penned nearly eight hundred years ago introduce the stories that follow and indicate how much more remains untold:

> Of all that God has shown me
> I can speak but the smallest word,
> Not more than a honey bee
> Takes on her foot
> From an overspilling jar. . . .[1]

PROLOGUE:
THE MEMORY BOX

On the top shelf of my bedroom closet, inside a cardboard box and wrapped carefully in plain white tissue these past twenty-five years, lies a fabulous hand-made cotton sash emblazoned with unfamiliar coinage. It is stunningly colorful—all pinks and golds and greens embroidered in an intricate geometric pattern. Anyone seeing it knows immediately that this is something out of the ordinary, something from another culture, possibly another century, or maybe even something out of a fairy tale.

When I hold the cloth, light glints from the coins to carom off my bedroom wall, and when I lift it they make a soft tinkling sound. But more than light or sound or craft or color, it is the sash's fragrance that always captures me. It smells mysteriously sweet yet at the same time foreign, the smell of a faraway place, of unknown mountain herbs, perhaps, or ancient incense from a place of murmured incantation. One whiff, and all these memories are summoned on its scent.

$\mathcal{A}$WAKENING

Before the sun had fully elbowed her way over the low eastern hills, or the community had begun to stir, or the gardeners had arrived to tend the manicured grounds, a lone tribesman from the distant mountains of Laos appeared in the faint light and stood silently beneath the large tree that shades the front lawn of our motherhouse convent. He stood there for some time, peering upward into the gray-green branches. Only the tip of the tree, some fifty feet above him, was lit by the sun. The year was 1980 and the place a town in California more than eight thousand miles, and at least several centuries, removed from the homeland this man had left behind a mere two months earlier. His name was Nhia Bee, and only later did I learn the full story of how he had come to be there.

If others had been awake, they surely would have wondered what he, an unarmed hunter skilled in the ways of his ancestors, intended to do at that hour and at that place. Nhia Bee stood barely five feet tall. His small frame was muscular, compact. Barefoot, he easily scaled the tree that morning. He settled himself among its highest branches, where he stayed, silent and unmoving and for the most part unseen, for the whole length of that day. At dusk he descended quickly, hiding something under his shirt, and slipped into that sprawling convent building where I lived with dozens of other nuns. No one at the convent (or just about anywhere in the United States, at that time) understood the language this man spoke. We knew neither his culture nor his past, and we certainly could not fathom the recent series of events—beginning with a spurt of violence at an airport—that had led to his wrenching relocations from airport terminal to county jail cell to hospital psych ward to suburban Catholic convent.

Nhia Bee and his family were refugees from a small, faraway corner of Southeast Asia. He and his wife and five young children had been living in our convent for two extraordinary months. None of us wanted them to leave, but their time with us was nevertheless drawing to a close. The decision was neither ours nor theirs. Forces beyond all of us had destined them for resettlement in the American Midwest— Illinois, to be specific. The specifics, however, meant nothing to this family. Nhia Bee could neither read nor write. Until his arrival at our convent he had not known how to hold a pencil; holding his family together had consumed energy enough.

They were all leaving the next day.

The final day at the convent dawned, and after breakfast, Nhia Bee sought me out. He stood unmoving in the convent common room with Pheng, his eldest son, silently at his side. The middle children clustered behind Pheng, while the younger ones clung shyly to Nhia's legs. Their mother, Seng, stayed several paces behind the others, not looking up, fidgeting with her shawl. Nhia then bowed and solemnly presented me with the fluttering gray mourning dove he had snared ever so-gently while in the tree. It was a farewell gift, a gift of peace. This was his wordless way of thanking my community for having cared for his family in their time of need.

Showing us a few grains of rice and miming the drinking of water, Nhia Bee indicated how we should feed this bird. Pheng cleverly slit a cardboard box to fashion a makeshift cage. The dove stepped nicely to and fro inside the carton, cooing softly, tilting its head this way and that, poking its beak through the slits, as unaware as I of how utterly my careful convent life was about to change because of Nhia Bee and his family.

A few hours later I stood at San Francisco's International Airport, the very place where our adventure had begun. A small contingent of nuns had come with me to see them off. Nhia Bee stood apart, his brow furrowed with anxiety. Seng, his wife, wept openly. Their children—Pheng, Xia, Ong, Chai, and Yeng—hung on to us affectionately, not understanding why they had to go. I barely understood it myself, for refugee resettlement was something strange and unknown to me back then.

Too soon, it was time for them to board the plane. Seng dug into her small cloth satchel and pulled out a dazzlingly bright handmade sash, its pinks and golds and greens dancing in the warm light. I had never seen anything like it. Still crying, she motioned me closer and tied the sash around my waist as if to bind us together. Only much later, when working in a refugee camp on the Lao border, did I realize that this must have been Seng's wedding sash; but it was instantly clear on this sad departure day that she was gifting me with her most precious possession.

"You'd better be careful," my best friend said, smiling wryly, trying to ease the heavy-heartedness we all felt. "I think this means you're betrothed to Nhia Bee. Maybe you're already his second wife."

The truth was more profound: This whole family was lodged in my heart.

Their plane departed, and we returned to the motherhouse convent, which now seemed too quiet without the playful noise and laughter of the children. The mourning dove we released that same day from its cardboard cage, watching it circle above the trees before lifting effortlessly on the breeze to perch atop the chapel roof. The sash, however, I kept. Even today, a full quarter-century later, its fragrance draws me into their world.

I stumbled into that strange world innocently enough. One day, two months earlier, I'd noticed a small card posted on our convent bulletin board outside the chapel, pinned crookedly to the cork amid the usual assortment of reminders: "Vespers will be at 5:30 p.m." and "please sign up to attend next Thursday's lecture" and a litany of prayer requests for the healing of aunt Tillie's broken hip and a successful job interview for Sister Raymond's nephew. The note said:

> *Urgent! Refugees arriving at SFO from Southeast Asia.*
> *Volunteers needed to assist at the International Terminal.*

The note piqued my curiosity. I had never met a refugee, though I had seen articles about them in the newspaper since the end of the Vietnam War. Thousands, I'd read, were fleeing Vietnam, Laos, and Cambodia. The United Nations was warehousing them in camps throughout Thailand, Malaysia, Indonesia, and Hong Kong. The camps sported exotic names like Palau Bidong, Ban Vinai, Phanat Nikhom, Khao-i-dang, and Nong Khai. All of them worlds away from the convent where I lived and worked. I was oblivious to the fact that Congress was drafting the "Refugee Act of 1980," which would formalize refugee resettlement, and that even now, two chartered 747s filled with refugees were landing daily at the San Francisco Airport, barely five miles from where I stood reading this note.

I was intrigued. I had been a high school teacher for seven years and had worked in inner-city Los Angeles, where simply showing up for class promised excitement. It was the sort of place where schoolyard scuffles involved knives. Gangs were a fact of life. On the first parent-teacher night, one of my colleagues commented to a young mother that her sophomore daughter seemed to be a gang member—only to have her teacherly concern trumped by the mother's steely-eyed reply: "So what? So am I."

Our convent was broken into six times during the four years I lived in LA. During one drive-by shooting, a machine gun was thrown over our fence, landing with a muffled thump in the ivy at the foot of a saint's statue. I grew accustomed to the searchlights from police helicopters lighting up our backyard at night. For all its difficulties, truth be told, I rather liked working there.

I was transferred from that setting, however, back to the Bay Area in order to do some administrative work for the religious congregation to which I belong. That meant relocating to our pristine motherhouse, situated on a forty-acre, picture-perfect campus named "The Oaks," for the five-hundred-year-old trees whose massive branches arch and lean above the sloping lawns and carefully tended gardens. The property holds a four-story convent, a retirement home, an administrative building, and a Tudor mansion long since transformed into a girls' secondary school. I love the serenity of the campus. It is holy ground for me, the place where I received my religious training and professed my vows of poverty, chastity, and obedience in the service of the poor. However, my administrative assignment, to put it plainly, was rather dull. I was very quickly looking for something more engaging to do during my free time.

And so this odd note on the bulletin board asking for volunteers found in me a receptive reader. I enlisted two friends, and we drove over to the airport that same afternoon to see what was happening.

Nothing could have prepared us for what we saw when the sliding glass doors parted and we walked into the airport. The central lobby of the international terminal had morphed into one solid expanse of humanity, but not of your typical air travelers. To begin with, no one was standing. Nearly everyone was squatting on the polished tile floor, and every face was Asian. The atmosphere was eerily subdued—no sounds except for some coughing and the soft crying of infants. Barebottomed toddlers crawled about, seemingly unsupervised. None of the older children or adults were conversing. All were in various stages of exhaustion; that much was obvious. Most of them, disturbingly thin, were wearing flimsy cotton trousers and T-shirts and had rubber thongs on their feet. Some leaned against one another or slept curled on the floor. Those who were awake squatted and shivered in the air-conditioned space.

The lobby looked incongruously like the photos I had seen in news magazines of distant refugee camps. Each family clutched a blue-and-white plastic bag, on which was written the family's name and serial number in bold, black ink. Scattered among the crowd on the floor were small boxes, some cobbled together from bamboo or cloth, some from battered cardboard tied with twine to protect whatever they contained.

As my friends and I surveyed the general chaos, we noticed a few Americans threading their way through the cramped scene, squinting at the names and numbers on those plastic bags. Occasionally one of them would stop and, through a series of hand motions, induce a few refugees to rise to their feet and follow. The selected ones would then uncrumple themselves from their tired neighbors and parade slowly out toward another terminal.

We had no idea what was going on.

Soon one of the Americans spotted us and pointed toward a small office on the far side of the lobby. We stepped our way gingerly over airsick children and sleeping torsos toward the office. Once inside, we could see that this was "command central." Two of the four walls were covered with large sheets of paper, and each sheet contained a long, handwritten list of airlines, flight numbers, gates, departure times, Asian names, and serial numbers identifying the cases (that is, families), as well as the number of persons in each case and the country through which they had been processed (Thailand, Indonesia, Malaysia, etc.). The lists on the walls displayed at least a hundred such rows of information, each row representing a clot of refugees on the floor of the lobby. I could see that the lists were in chronological order for flights scheduled to depart that day:

FLIGHT	GATE	TIME	FAMILY	CASE #
Delta #592	03	1226	Triet-Nguyen Vo (7)	IN- 000349
AA #829	64	1315	Chhunhakk Ranariddh (1)	T- 000082
UA #175	25	1330	Nguyen Thi Truong (5)	M-000714

A petite, energetic Asian woman immediately approached us.

"Volunteers?" she asked. The expression on her face made it clear there was only one correct answer to the question.

"Probably," I said, grinning.

"Excellent! Just memorize a row of information from the top of the list, put a check mark in the margin so we'll know you're working on that case, and go find the corresponding family—out there," she said, sweeping her arm broadly toward the throng in the lobby. "Take them through x-ray, out to the departure gate, and onto the plane. Buckle their seat belts and say good-bye. Then come back here, find the next departure, and repeat the steps for as long as you can stay."

In my naiveté, I thought the hard part would be memorizing the information from the list so that I could actually find a family and begin the process. Little did I know. But before I launched into action, I needed a bit more context and background.

"Uh, where exactly are these people going?" I asked, still not comprehending the big picture. "And why?"

"They've just arrived from Southeast Asia on a twenty-two hour flight. Now they have to catch their connecting flights to their final destinations," explained the woman, whose name I learned was Jade. "The federal government is bringing them in. Churches and other organizations throughout the country are waiting to resettle them. Seven hundred of them are landing here every day on charter flights from the camps. We have only three staff, and as you can see we are swamped, so we've put out an all-call for volunteers."

Later I learned that Jade's *we* referred to the International Organization for Migration (IOM), the agency to whom the United Nations subcontracts the global task of health screenings for refugees overseas and the monumental responsibility of booking them on flights and ensuring that they reach their correct destinations safely; and to the US Catholic Conference (USCC), the largest agency involved in welcoming and resettling refugees in the United States.

I cannot recall the faces of the families I shepherded onto flights that afternoon and evening, though I do clearly remember how hopelessly inept I felt. First off, it was not easy in that ragged patchwork of people to find the one family whose name and serial number matched the data I'd memorized. To my sheltered Anglo brain, all the names looked more or less identical and equally unpronounceable. Being a math teacher, I decided to concentrate instead on the serial numbers. Each time I found a match, I experienced a fleeting moment of self-satisfaction, akin to solving a niggling clue in a *New York Times* crossword puzzle. Then came the anxious realization that, according to my watch, I had less than twenty-five minutes to get this family to their connecting flight before it departed. Frantic pantomimes ensued. Point to their name on the plastic UN bag. Smile. Point to the family members. Point to myself. Smile again. Usher them up into a standing position. Three minutes gone; twenty-two remaining.

Once the family was erect and following me, I escorted them to an adjacent terminal. I use the term "adjacent" loosely: The distances were significant. "Hurry, hurry," I'd whisper urgently to them, knowing full well they couldn't understand English. But even if they had understood my words, the very concept of hurrying, so central to my life, would not have been particularly meaningful to them. Especially not now, when they were exhausted and didn't know where they were or where they were going next or why there was any need to move quickly. Though they followed me without complaining, I simply could not convince them to move their rubber-thonged feet with anything approximating haste. Whenever I turned around to make sure they were still with me, I'd see they had dropped twenty paces farther behind. Another ten minutes gone; twelve remaining.

The next hurdle was the x-ray station. Understandably, the refugees did not wish to be separated from their meager possessions, not even for a minute, and certainly not onto a moving belt that disappeared into a black box. More frantic hand demonstrations: "See? It's OK. There goes my purse. I get it back on the other side. No problem."

For the refugees, of course, this wasn't true. Lumpy packages of herbs or medicines were rejected. Homemade knives proved troublesome. The screeners, mostly unperturbed in those pre-9/11 days, took it all in stride and explained to me how the offending items could be mailed to the refugees' final destinations. The refugees, however, could not know this. For them, it was one more loss in a string of heavy losses: my land, my livelihood, my language, my extended family, my culture; and now, my dagger—so essential for hunting, defending my family, cooking and, of course, building my next home, wherever this long journey was taking me.

In retrospect, I wonder why they didn't simply refuse to part with these small things—these last precious remnants of home—that they had clutched while fleeing from war and then had borne all the way to this strange new world. What kept them from calling a literal halt to this madness and deciding they had walked far enough already, lost too much already, taken in too much strangeness already? Perhaps sheer exhaustion made them compliant, or perhaps they kept moving for the sake of their children. At the time those questions were not in my head—I knew only that five more minutes had evaporated; seven remained.

Onward to the departure gate. Ah, a moveable sidewalk! This should help. Guiding a family onto the conveyor was simple enough; they seemed pleased and amazed—and probably relieved that I had finally stopped prodding them to move faster. Getting off was another matter. I strode ahead, to demonstrate how it was done. By the time I looked over my shoulder, it was too late. The sidewalk had ended but the refugees' momentum had not, toppling the whole family onto one another. Five minutes gone; only two remaining. I left them there to untangle themselves as I bolted for the gate, begging the airline attendant, "Hold the plane!" while the family slowly regrouped and approached. The airline personnel complied, no doubt frozen by the sight of a nun in habit, arms flailing, flagging them down.

All of this must have been incomprehensible to the refugees themselves, who were probably wondering if this strange new place would ever make any sense. In my sense of urgency, I had not even introduced myself to them, I am ashamed to say. My single moment of interpersonal exchange, of actually relating to these families as human beings, occurred after the refugees were on the plane with their seat belts fastened. Then I would take a deep breath and look each one in the eye as I murmured a quick farewell. The plane's engines were already revving, so there was no time to linger. I dashed for the door, thanking the flight attendants as I retreated, and retraced my steps back to the lobby of the main terminal, to repeat this bizarre sequence.

After that first day, I realized how much more efficient it would be to recruit and organize additional volunteers. This was easy enough to do for someone in my position, first among the nuns and then the high school girls from our motherhouse campus. Soon I had mustered and oriented fifty or so volunteers and assigned them various time slots for helping the overstressed IOM staff. The younger nuns joined me on airport duty; the older ones handled kitchen detail. We discovered that the refugees had no food to eat during their long layovers (other than what they'd been offered on the airplane, which was hardly identifiable to them as food). USCC was willing to provide food but couldn't imagine what that might be. It had to be portable, nutritious, inexpensive, and recognizable to the refugees.

"What about hard-boiled eggs?" I suggested to the airport staff.

"Wonderful idea," agreed Jade, "but where are we going to find fifty dozen hard-boiled eggs every day?"

The older nuns rolled up their sleeves: Six hundred raw eggs were delivered into the motherhouse kitchen every afternoon, and six hundred hard-boiled eggs were carted out to the airport lobby at dawn the next morning. The high school girls proved to be the best recruits.

Accustomed to baby-sitting, they instinctively knew that what we really needed was diapers, lots of diapers, to slap onto the infants and toddlers because the shiny tile of the airport lobby, unlike the dirt in the refugee camps, absorbed neither "number one" nor "number two". School was in session, of course, but the students volunteered in three-hour shifts at all the other hours between 5:00 a.m. and 10:00 p.m. They were simply wonderful, escorting families to the planes, entertaining sick children, helping overtired parents to cope. We kept this up for several months, until IOM had managed to hire a full contingent of staff for its considerable daily workload.

Inevitably, there were families who missed their flights. Whenever anyone needed to use the restroom, for example, the entire twenty or thirty minutes of available escort time could disappear while the family assessed our western toilets, their faces scrunched in wordless dismay: *Sit on this? You've got to be kidding! That's disgusting; how many other people have already sat here . . . ?* It made much more sense to them to stand on the toilet seat and squat. They had their point, and later, when I went overseas to work in a refugee camp, it was my turn to learn the proper use of a squat toilet.

Whenever a family missed their plane, we'd wind our way back to command central and ask IOM to rebook them on another flight and notify the personnel expecting to receive the family at the point of final destination.

Rebooking wasn't always doable within the same day, in which case the family needed to be transported to a nearby motel for an overnight stay. That entailed more adventures: convincing the refugees that water from the tap in their motel room was drinkable, showing them how to blend the spray in the shower to a temperature that would not scald, demonstrating how to use the bed—usually by physically lifting the youngest child and stuffing him or her between the sheets, evoking peals of laughter from the rest of the family—and convincing them that they must stay in that motel room until a staff member retrieved them the next day. Never having been particularly good at "charades," it was quite a revelation to me that so much could be explained without actually using words.

Sometimes the refugees missed their connections for more serious reasons. One tired serial number lying limp on the terminal floor turned out to be to a semi-conscious refugee, delirious with fever and chills. That night, after driving him to the nearest hospital whose staff knew something about tropical diseases, I added dengue fever to my vocabulary. What to do with special cases like this? I decided to bring them home to our convent until they were travel-ready. It seemed the most expedient solution.

At that time, however, our motherhouse was "for nuns only." It was outside the norm to bring in anyone, much less a refugee—much, *much* less a *male* refugee at 11:00 at night—but that is what I did. After the initial shock of it, the community members rallied; they were patient with me and very welcoming of our new charges. The convent became IOM's fallback plan for the occasional adult refugee whose situation required an overnight stay that couldn't be accommodated in the regular motel. Over time, it brought out the best in all of us, for the spirit of our particular religious order is mercy, nothing more and nothing less than responding in practical ways to needs that are known. The motherhouse, being more physically isolated than our other convents where nuns ministered in various neighborhoods, was enriched by the presence of these strangers suddenly in our midst.

And so it happened one Saturday afternoon, while I was busily engaged at a two-day community meeting, that the portress delivered a message from Jade: *Urgent. Please call.* I'd already explained to Jade that I wouldn't be available on this particular weekend due to the meeting, so I wondered what her call was about. At the coffee break I reached her by phone.

"Sister, please, we have a special case. Can you take in a mother and five children?" Without waiting for a reply, she continued, "I'll bring them over in an hour."

Then she hung up. I laughed; what else could I do?

The day was unusually chilly for California; rain was falling steadily. I stared out a window, and from my sheltered indoor vantage point, I remember thinking that the downpour made the grassy slopes and old oak trees look even lovelier than usual. I now realize—after having lived a year in Thailand—that "cold" and "rain" are words that simply do not go together in Southeast Asia, and that our dreary weather must only have added to the refugees' feelings of complete disorientation.

A little over an hour later, when my meeting had adjourned, I walked out of the motherhouse gathering room, down a long corridor, up a flight of stairs, past the chapel, and into the carpeted front lobby of the convent. There stood Jade waiting for me, surrounded by a sad little huddle of rain-soaked figures. Six refugees were there in all—wet, trembling from the cold, and, judging by the wide-eyed looks on their set faces, absolutely petrified.

"There's been a problem with their father," said Jade. "He's being detained by the police. Keep the family here a few days until we can get it straightened out, OK? I'll call you as soon as we learn more details."

Then she added, "Oh, by the way, they're Hmong and we haven't been able to find anyone who speaks their language."

Off she zipped in her car back to the airport, leaving me standing there, staring at this forlorn and now fatherless family.

Hmong? What was that?

A New Way of Loving

Jewish Hasidim tell the story of a rabbi's child who used to walk alone in the dark woods. At first the rabbi let his son wander, but over time he grew concerned. The woods, after all, were dangerous; the father did not know what lurked there. He decided to discuss the matter with his child. One day he took him aside and said, "You know, I have noticed that each day you walk into the woods. I wonder why you go there."

The boy said, "I go there to find God."

"That is a very good thing," the father replied gently. "I am glad that you are searching for God. But, my child, don't you know that God is the same everywhere?"

"Yes," the boy answered, "but I'm not."[1]

For that same reason, I suppose, as much as any other, God invited me to step into the world of refugees.

The refugees, Nhia Bee's wife, Seng, and their children—Pheng, Xia, Ong, Chai, and Yeng, ages fourteen, twelve, ten, six, and one year old, respectively—eyed me guardedly, rainwater dripping with their tears onto the red-carpeted motherhouse lobby. They did not know where Nhia Bee had been taken. They did not know whether they would ever see him again. They did know—as I was to learn later—that Nhia Bee had been in a fight that left another man seriously injured, and that police had removed him from the scene in handcuffs, after which Jade brought his family to our convent. They were, as Jade had said earlier, Hmong: A proud, fiercely independent ethnic group from the rugged mountains of Laos, mostly preliterate but skilled in slash-and-burn farming. During the Vietnam war era, the Hmong formed the backbone of the CIA's mostly secret side-war in Laos; after 1975, when US forces pulled out of that corner of southeast Asia, the triumphant communist Pathet Lao hunted the Hmong with a fury, causing thousands to flee their mountains for the first time ever, escaping across the Mekong and into refugee camps in Thailand. Having known only thatch huts, I cannot imagine what the family must have thought of their sudden insertion into our huge convent with its one hundred and fifty rooms.

I led the family up the stairs to a fourth-floor corridor behind the chapel organ gallery. There I pointed out the five bedrooms I'd reserved for them. Convent bedrooms, formerly known as cells, are small in size, with just enough space to fit one single bed, a small desk and sink, and a narrow closet designed to hold two black habits—nothing more. This was not really a problem for Nhia Bee's family because, as it turned out, they had no possessions other than three shoebox-sized cardboard boxes tied with string.

I showed them where to find the bathrooms and the stairwell that led down to the dining area. Pheng, the eldest, was doing his best to head up the family in the absence of his father and in these puzzling new surroundings. Though he knew no English, he spoke to his

mother and siblings in their own language every time I said or panto-
mimed anything. Who knows for sure what he told them? His face told
me nothing.

The next morning I went to retrieve them for breakfast and was
alarmed to see that four of the five bedrooms had not been touched.
All six family members were piled together in one tiny room, having pulled the mattress onto the floor. At the time, of course, I had no
idea that privacy is not a core value in all cultures, or that the American concept of personal space meant little to the Hmong. Only later would I learn that for those who live in poverty, especially those
outside the Western world, there is really no such thing as separate
bedrooms. For the nine wonderful weeks they lived at the Oaks, the
family never used more than that one tiny ten-by-twelve room.

The children settled in quickly and soon transformed our quiet
convent with their spontaneity. We taught the older children a bit of
English each day and shared in the exuberance of their many discov-
eries: the miracles of toaster and doorbell and elevator and running
water; the television with its amazing remote control; the odd food,
gratefully accepted, but with astonishment—rice was not served at
every meal? When the children figured out how to work the in-house
telephone extensions, they exploded with delight. Supposing that this
marvel worked only in English, they spoke over and over again the
phrases they had learned, laughing uncontrollably all the while. They
played outside and wrestled with one another on the lawn and clambered on the limbs of our lovely oaks. They fell asleep in our arms
whenever we went for an outing in the car.

We took them to the aquarium in San Francisco, where they ran
from tank to tank pointing out the colored fish. It was all we could
do to pull them away at closing time. They sat glum-faced and silent
during the ride home. Only later did we realize that they thought we
had gone there to select their dinner. We went on shopping forays for
shoes (a novelty) and basic clothing. Twelve-year-old Xia showed up
for breakfast the next morning wearing only her new cotton slip—she

informed us that it was so pretty that she didn't want to cover it with her new dress. We had to grab fourteen-year-old Pheng before he headed out the door wearing only his new Jockey under-shorts to play soccer with the high school girls. And how they all loved the bathtubs! While the community was in the chapel early each morning for meditation, the splish-splashing and squealing of the children drifted happily down from behind the choir loft.

Meals and bedtime brought joys as well. Our community of nuns eats dinner in common at the Oaks, and ten-year-old Ong quickly learned that if he cleared the Sisters' dishes from the table after dinner, he could be the ice cream server. Serving ice cream for several tables, he discovered he could join each table and enjoy dessert over and over. Chai, the family's irrepressible six-year-old, stole my heart from the beginning. When I sat down to read him stories in the evening, he would climb onto my lap, snuggle up as close as he could, then pull my arms around him into a tight hug and gently bend my head down until we were cheek to cheek and I could rock him for a while. Things got a bit more serious when the baby, Yeng, came down with chicken pox and we had to begin a series of visits to various medical clinics. Gradually, the family adjusted to life in "the big house," and we adjusted along with them.

A few days after their coming, we learned that Nhia Bee had indeed been locked up in a local jail for attacking a volunteer with a length of metal pipe.[2] To this day, Nhia Bee has no memory of the incident and can only surmise that he was feverish and confused after the long flight from Asia. When he realized that he and his family were being escorted by uniformed personnel from the airport, he most likely thought that they were being taken captive, and so he struck out in an effort to protect them.

Once jailed, Nhia Bee assumed that he would be killed by "the authorities" for having injured an American. To avoid the shame of that, he attempted suicide in his jail cell, whereupon his jailers transferred him to the psychiatric ward of a nearby hospital. Sadly, all of

this transpired with no interpreter available. He was alone throughout this ordeal.

When Jade informed me of this pitiful chain of events, I immediately drove Seng to the hospital to visit her husband. What neither of
us knew until we entered Nhia Bee's room was that he was being kept
in restraints, tied to the bed, considered by the doctors to be a danger to himself and others. I was as horrified as Seng at the sight of him
bound and immobilized. I pleaded with the doctors to untie him and
let him go free. After much whispered discussion among themselves,
the doctors finally allowed him out of bed. As Nhia Bee walked slowly
up and down the hospital corridor with Seng at his side, his face a por-
trait of bewilderment, I continued advocating with the medical professionals for his discharge. *No way*, I was told. *Too dangerous.*

Certainly, these professionals were doing their jobs. Given what
they knew of Nhia Bee's behavior outside the airport, they had to consider him a dangerous man. And because of the language barrier, they
were unable to discover his motivations or his mindset. They had to
keep him restrained while they figured out how to treat his case.

But once I saw him in person and watched his face soften with affection at the sight of his wife, I felt immediately that Nhia Bee was not
a deliberately violent man. Something about the tender way he gazed
at Seng, followed by the silent, pleading look he directed toward me,
convinced me that this was all a terrible mistake.

I called refugee processing headquarters in New York City and ar-
gued for his release: "Let Nhia Bee come to stay with his family at our
convent. I have seen this man's eyes; he is not going to hurt anyone."

"Sorry," came the answer. "That would be recklessly putting the
nuns' lives in danger."

"No! Trust me; this has been a terrible ordeal, but it can't be cor-
rected in a hospital." Day after day, I stubbornly chipped away at their
resolve to hold him as an inpatient. After Nhia Bee had spent several
weeks on the psych ward (all the while without an interpreter), the
doctors finally—and very reluctantly—released him to our care.

When Nhia Bee reunited with his family at our convent, the children swarmed over him, hugging and crying and laughing. The anxiety that had lined his face during his weeks of confinement melted quickly away as he played with them and stroked their heads and listened to their stories. Then he went upstairs with Seng, motioning for me to follow. From one of the family's little cardboard boxes he pulled out something heavy, wrapped in fabric. He unfolded the faded gray cloth to reveal a bamboo sheath from which he pulled a metal dagger, obviously hand-fashioned. He bowed low, held out both hands with palms upraised, and ceremoniously presented the knife to me. No doubt this was his most valuable possession—perhaps his only possession. Any shred of worry that this man might harbor a violent streak evaporated with that gesture. We became fast friends.

Still, Nhia Bee was required to see the doctors in San Francisco every week for the next four weeks. I sympathized with their dilemma. Here was a stranger from a place and culture these professionals knew little about, a man who had inexplicably lashed out with a piece of metal pipe, inflicting injury on an American volunteer, and then attempted suicide. What was going on in Nhia Bee's mind? How was he interpreting his surroundings? Might he behave in ways that would put others or himself in danger again?

The truth was, Nhia Bee was one of the gentlest men I had ever met. Officials in New York phoned me regularly: *How were we* (the Sisters) *doing? Did we feel safe? Would we mind keeping the family until the doctors felt more confident that he was stable?* I chafed at the implication that Nhia Bee was some sort of unpredictable lunatic—though I had to admit that his behavior at the airport gave ample reason to draw that conclusion.

At the same time, I was secretly and quite selfishly glad about the professionals' continued caution: It meant that the whole family might stay with us longer.

Inevitably the day arrived when the medical experts confirmed what we who lived with him had long felt: Nhia Bee was fine. He and his family were cleared for travel to the church group sponsoring them in the Midwest. And so we bade our sad farewells at the airport in April with images of doves and wedding sashes, soccer scrimmages and bedtime stories and ice-cream-loving mini-waiters brimming up behind our own tears.

It turned out that this was the beginning, not the end, of my life with refugees. Several months later, as my administrative assignment at the motherhouse was coming to a close and I was planning to return to high school teaching, I had a dream. Not a vision or a prophetic utterance—just an ordinary dream, in the middle of an ordinary night like any other, a night that gave no hint of being auspicious.

In my dream I was standing in a large schoolyard. My arms were full of books. The bell for class was ringing. Suddenly, at the far side of the yard, I spied Nhia Bee's five children. They saw me at the same instant and came running. I dropped my books and scooped up six-year-old Chai into a bear hug. I felt deliriously happy at seeing them. They all crowded around me, and I squatted down to greet each of them. I had not seen or talked to them since they'd flown off to Illinois.

"What are you doing here?" I asked.

Impishly, Chai grinned back, "We're here to teach you a new way of loving."

With those words I awakened. It may sound strange, but when I awoke I was convinced that this was an invitation from God to involve myself full-time in refugee work. I immediately felt a tremendous surge of happiness and energy. Shortly thereafter, I followed my heart's prompting and committed to spending a year working in a Lao refugee camp in Thailand. There I would learn that the name *Chai* means "heart".

Several years later, when I was back in the San Francisco Bay Area, I heard that Nhia Bee and his family had relocated to California's Central Valley. I drove to see them and stayed overnight in their small apartment, sleeping on a mattress they arranged for me on the floor. For breakfast, Seng sizzled garlic and fish in a large frying pan. The television blared a cowboy Western. The children's English was now fluent, so we were able to converse at length for the first time. We sat together and talked and laughed about their memories of "the Sisters' big house." Suddenly, in the middle of a sentence, Pheng jumped up from the couch and slammed off the television with his hand.

"What's the matter?" I asked. "Don't you like cowboy movies?"

"Sure," he replied, "but you have to be very careful. When the cowboys point their guns toward us, the bullets can come out and we might get killed." He, the eldest son, was carefully protecting his younger siblings. After three years in the United States, the family still struggled to find the line between what was real and what was not in this perplexing new land.

That summer I invited the four oldest children to vacation with me near Lake Tahoe. We stayed in a cabin at a 6,000-foot elevation in El Dorado National Forest. What an experience! After all, the Hmong are mountain people; this family had been starved for mountains since their US arrival. We spent several glorious days hiking through forests of pine, fir, and incense cedar. The children bombarded me with questions: "What is the name of this plant? Is this berry poisonous? What sicknesses will this leaf cure?"

I confessed that I didn't know any of the answers. They stopped walking to stare at me in disbelief: "You *live* here, don't you?" Still they plied me for information: "What about wild animals? How do you catch them? Are there any farms? Can we stay here all the time?"

They were ecstatic at seeing their first mountain creek. Though surprised by the coldness—it was snowmelt, after all—they waded right in and got busy. With sticks and leaves the older boys constructed a partial dam, and then stood to the side of it, legs apart and motionless, staring into the fast-moving current. I thought they were playing.

I was wrong.

After standing immobile for quite some time, Pheng and Ong suddenly scooped their bare hands into the icy water and emerged with shouts of triumph, clenching slippery, wriggling trout! My mouth dropped open in sheer amazement.

The next day we chanced upon some national park rangers standing on a bridge, dumping barrels full of trout into the south fork of the American River. Now it was the children's turn to be dumbfounded: "What are they doing?" I explained that the men were stocking the river so that people could enjoy fishing. Xia turned to me, incredulous: "Why don't they just *give* the fish to the people?"

Again I had no satisfactory reply, but by this time in my life, I was learning to hold things more lightly, to laugh at life's incongruities, and to view the world from more perspectives than my own suburban upbringing had previously allowed. By this time, I had begun my new way of loving and was more at home with a world of paradoxes, mysteries, and unanswered questions.

As romantic as a "new way of loving" may sound, it has in fact been a rather humbling experience. Through my subsequent relationships with refugees from so many parts of the world, my ways of thinking have continually been brought up short.

To begin with, there is the American fixation with time. Like most Americans, I absorbed this precision even before I could read. School started at 8:20; recess spanned exactly 9:55 to 10:10. As I grew older, I accepted without question the peculiar notions that time is money and that it is the height of rudeness to keep anyone waiting. Then I moved to rural Thailand to work in Nong Khai refugee camp.

On my first free weekend, I decided to take the bus to Udon Thani, some thirty miles south of Nong Khai. Locals told me that the bus would be at the marketplace on Saturday morning. I pressed them for a specific time. Maybe around 8:00 a.m., they told me, shrugging. I arrived exactly at 8:00 and climbed aboard, dictionary in hand, to negotiate the fare with the driver. There were two other passengers: one older woman carrying a basket of fruit, and a young man holding two live chickens. I smiled at them and the chickens and settled into my seat. Then I waited. And waited. A full hour passed. Then another. Meanwhile, several other passengers had joined us. The bus, which had been comfortable in the morning light, was now stiflingly hot. The chickens were restless, and so was I. Finally, having cobbled together my question from the Lao phrase book, I approached the driver. I asked him, as politely as I could, "When. Will. The. Bus. Leave?" He seemed surprised by the question. "When it gets *full*," he said.

Later that year, during a visit to southern Thailand with another nun, I learned something about personal space. We needed to take a taxi in order to reach a village not served by any buses. We approached a Toyota sedan parked nearby. I stepped back when I saw that the car was already full. In the front seat—besides the driver—sat two men, one of them carrying live roosters. In the back seat were two women (substantial packages on their laps) along with three small children. My companion opened the back door and motioned for me to get in. I didn't see anywhere to sit. While I hesitated, the women and children obligingly scrunched over to create a space. Dubious, I squeezed in, and then watched in amazement as the other sister (who had lived in Thailand for many years) piled in behind me. Before I could say anything, two more men entered the front seat from the other side, forcing the earlier occupants to straddle the gear shift box. Now we were twelve!

The driver, to make room, opened his own door and shifted his body almost completely out of the vehicle. But he didn't start the engine. He continued studiously cleaning his fingernails with a pen knife. The other nun then exchanged a few quick sentences with him in Thai that I didn't understand. He thanked her, put away the knife, revved up the engine and sped off on the dirt road, driving with his door still wide open and most of his body hanging outside. Only one foot and arm remained inside the taxi. He careened along the rutted road, using only horn and accelerator while passing huge trucks like some steroid-crazed leapfrog, as if making up for the taxi's small size with his bravado. I held my breath—there was hardly room to breathe anyway—and prayed. Only when we had finally reached our destination, exited the cab, and paid the driver did I ask my companion what she had said to him at the outset.

"I told him I'd pay for the extra fare so that you wouldn't feel crowded."

"What extra fare?" I asked, restraining myself from commenting on the "so I wouldn't feel crowded."

"No taxi will start until it has ten paying passengers aboard," she explained, "and children don't count."

Another revelation was the significance of rank and seniority in many cultures. My democratized American brain considers everyone to be equal. It's simply a given for me, a starting place for social interaction. Not so in Asia or Africa.

The standard greeting in Thailand is a slight bow, accompanied by the *wai*, palms pressed together in a prayer position, as you say "*Sa wa dee kah!*" Etiquette requires that the *wai* be adjusted according to the status of the person you are greeting. To say hello to a child, perform the gesture so that the tips of the fingers touch your own chin. For a peer, put your hands in front of your face, touching your nose. For a superior (anyone who is even one day older, or anyone of greater social importance) the tips of your fingers must be pointing toward the top of your forehead.

In Thailand the head is considered to be the sacred location of the soul, and therefore a person of lower status (for example, a child) will always keep his head below the level of any older person's head. This explained the constant ducking and stooping that occurred as people passed one another. It was especially awkward when the elder was seated, since it necessitated deep crouching in order to move past him or her. To this day I still retain this habit; when forced to walk between two people—say, in the hallway of an office—I'll duck quickly and murmur, "Excuse me," but what I'm really thinking is "*kaw toht*," the reverent Lao apology.

This cultural practice was dramatically displayed on the day the Thai king's son got married. The brief Buddhist ceremony was broadcast live throughout Thailand, and the whole country came to a halt to watch it wherever there was a television. The king was seated on a low cushion, so naturally his head was quite low. When the prince and his bride-to-be entered the hallway, arrayed in royal splendor, they literally crawled on their bellies up the full length of the room to greet the king! The ceremony lasted only a few minutes but left an unforgettable impression on me.

Years later, during a time when I was the manager of a large refugee resettlement office in California, I asked Musa, one of our new employees and a refugee from Sierra Leone, to please set up the conference room for a routine staff meeting. All I wanted him to do was to drag a few tables together into a square and arrange chairs around them. This he did, but then he approached one of the other team members with a question.

"Where is Sister's chair?" he asked.

"What are you talking about? Sister doesn't have a special chair."

He ran off and asked another colleague, "Where can I find Sister's chair?" but got the same response. He began to sweat, thinking that his co-workers did not like him and were trying to get him fired. Frantic, he returned to ask me directly, "Please, where may I find your chair?"

I was in a hurry, so I answered him rather brusquely, saying that I would sit anywhere—just fix the room with fifteen chairs. Now he was sure that he was going to lose his job. He ran from person to person, begging to be shown where the Director's chair was kept, all to no avail, except that his co-workers were beginning to wonder about his sanity.

We held our usual staff meeting that afternoon, sitting around the conference tables. Musa remained silent for the entire hour, as wide-eyed and tensed as a cornered animal. Afterward, he again came to me to apologize for not having set up the right chair. I asked, a bit exasperated, what in the world he was talking about. After hesitating a minute, perhaps trying to decide if this were a trick question that could lead to his dismissal, he explained that, of course, the Chief always had a designated chair that was carved and decorated and much larger than any other chair in the village. Only the Chief could use it. No Chief in Africa would ever use anything less. Musa assumed that it must be the same in America. Even when I assured him that I was not a Chief and would never require special seating, it was a long while before Musa completely lost the look of someone nearly brought before a firing squad.

One year Musa joined my family for Thanksgiving dinner. After the meal my father, a spry eighty-year-old, rose to help clear the plates and rinse them in the kitchen. A look of horror crossed Musa's face, but to his credit he also got up to help. He told me the next morning that he had never, ever seen a man work willingly in a kitchen, that it was especially unthinkable for an *elder* to do so, and never in his wildest dreams had he imagined that he would ever do it himself—but that he was learning this impossible etiquette by observing Americans in action.

One of the immediate goals for every refugee in America is to obtain a job. To that end, the refugee resettlement team prepares the newcomers for employment by assessing their work histories and transferable skills. Some refugees had been carpenters or tailors or teachers and could move after minimal retraining into the job market. But others were subsistence farmers or non-literate vendors, or they carried serious scars from war. It was much more challenging to prepare them for jobs.

One refugee who arrived with his pregnant wife had had his right arm chopped off by rebels during a West African war, ostensibly because he had voted "for the wrong candidate." He was, understandably, still deeply traumatized and having difficulty in his transition to life in America. My co-workers were coaching him daily on the reality facing him: "You will start at a low-paying job; but if you apply yourself, you will be able to work your way up the ladder over time." They explained that they would do their best to find him a job paying about eight dollars.

He objected strenuously, refusing to consider it even for a minute. "I will *not* take a job paying eight dollars! *Impossible!* I refuse to work for anything less than *twenty*!"

"Twenty?" The staff tried to reason with him. "Look, you have some handicaps; you have no work history here; your English skills are very minimal; you don't have a high school diploma. You will need to start at the bottom and be patient. Over time you will learn new skills and get a better-paying position."

He dug in his heels.

"I won't do it. I have calculated what I need for my family to survive, and I can't do it on less than twenty!" His manner was verging on hysteria.

At that point I intervened in the conversation in an attempt to calm him down. "OK, let's look at the numbers." I penciled it out for him on a sheet of paper: his monthly revenue, less taxes, at eight dollars per hour in a full-time job. Then I asked him to show me his estimated monthly expenses for rent, food, transportation, etc. He didn't budge. He was staring at the first number.

"What is that?" he asked.

"You can see it," I told him. "It will be your income for one month."

His eyes locked onto it for another minute or two. The fight seemed to have gone out of him entirely. He slumped slightly in his chair and then looked up at me apologetically. "Oh. I thought you meant eight dollars per day, not eight dollars per hour." The latter was a rate nearly inconceivable to him. He accepted the next job that was offered.

While living in Thailand, I was particularly bothered by one custom that I witnessed over and over: people blew their noses by holding one nostril closed and blowing out the other one, straight onto the ground. I found it disgusting but felt it would be impolite to mention it. A colleague, somewhat more assertive, directly asked one of the Thai men about this practice and told him how offensive it looked. The man immediately countered with his own rebuttal on the peculiar habits of Westerners: "Well, why do you people use a piece of tissue—snort, snort—and then carefully put it in your pocket? What are you saving it for?"

Notions of beauty also differ among cultures. One coming-of-age ritual for boys of the Dinka people in southern Sudan is the removal of several front teeth. I was involved in the resettlement in California of many Dinka refugees who had fled the civil war in Sudan, and most of them arrived gap-toothed. I asked one of them the reason for this custom, which, now that they were living in the States, left them at a disadvantage for enunciating certain English sounds clearly. The young man looked at me as if the reason were perfectly obvious to everyone: "Well," he said, "no girl would *ever* marry you if you had *all* your teeth!"

They were dismayed to learn that American women had different views on attractiveness. Many of the Dinka in the United States eventually turned themselves and their hard-earned dollars over to orthodontists.

Some of the refugees also suffer the indignity of having names that do not translate comfortably into English. *Dung,* for example, is a common Vietnamese name. I know an African man, so black he looks almost purple, whose given name is *Albino*. And another with the name *Ding Ding,* who named his sons *Ding Dong* and *Riing Ding.*

All of these things, small in themselves, heighten the refugees' self-consciousness about fitting in and succeeding in their new homeland. The unspoken norms governing relationships are painfully confusing. Is it OK for heterosexual males to hold hands in public, as is commonplace in some parts of Africa? What is the proper way to greet people? How can you make friends here? Who arranges marriages? How will dowries be paid where there are no cows? Most perplexing and tentative of all, naturally, are social interactions with the opposite gender. Where does one begin? What is appropriate? What is taboo?

One Christmas, a handsome twenty-year-old refugee from West Africa, Gerard by name, pulled me aside at a holiday gathering, anxious to talk privately.

"May I ask you a moral question?" he whispered.

Nodding, I said, "Of course."

"Is it OK to give a Christmas gift to a young woman through her grandmother?" Gerard looked distinctly ill-at-ease.

"Yes, of course," I replied. "I think that would be very appropriate."

"But I tried to do it this morning," said Gerard, "to a girl in the apartment adjacent to mine . . ."

"And . . . ?" I waited for him to continue.

". . . and her grandmother accepted the gift but then said loudly to me, 'Oh, Gerard, you *shouldn't* have done this!' Now I don't know if it was correct to give it to her or not. I'm afraid I did something quite wrong."

I explained, insofar as I could, that the grandmother's remark was meant as a gracious exaggeration, a way of saying thanks, certainly not as a reprimand. I presumed that Gerard was feeling chagrined by the perceived rebuff and was agonizing over how to approach the girl again. To set him at ease, I asked,

"So, how old is this young woman?"

"Three," answered Gerard.

His simple attempt to reach out to a child in a neighborly way on Christmas Day had left him mired in self-doubt. Much greater is the angst surrounding peer friendships and dating. Invariably, these are the areas most confusing to the refugees. Many times I have been asked, "Sister, how can we make new friends here?" The answer to that, I believe, lies not with the refugees but with the welcome (or lack of welcome) from the resident communities into which they arrive.

I'm grateful for the many ways the refugees have opened me to new ways of seeing and thinking, new understandings of diversity, new ways of loving. I'm different because of my interactions with them.

This prayer, attributed to Voltaire several centuries ago, now echoes my own:

> O thou God of all beings, of all worlds, and of all times,
> We pray,
> that the little differences
> in our clothes,
> in our inadequate languages,
> in our ridiculous customs,
> in our imperfect laws,
> in our illogical opinions,
> in our ranks and conditions, which
> are so disproportionately important to us
> and so meaningless to you,
> that these small variations
> that distinguish those atoms that we call men,
> one from another,
> may never be signals of hatred and persecution.[3]

This may require a new way of loving on the part of us all.

$\mathcal{G}$OD WHO $\mathcal{W}$EEPS

G. K. Chesterton tells the story of a person—let's call him Joe—who lived a rather unreflective life and was entirely indifferent to spiritual matters. Early in midlife, Joe unexpectedly died and slid unceremoniously into hell. Joe's old buddies really missed him. One evening, over a few beers, they formulated a plan to rescue him. They decided that Joe's business partner should go down to the gates of hell to negotiate springing him from the place. He knocked and knocked, pleaded and pleaded, but the gates never budged; the heavy iron bars stayed firmly shut.

Next, his parish priest went down and requested an appointment with Satan himself. He carefully laid out the case: "Look, Joe wasn't really such a terrible fellow. Given more time, it's possible that he might have matured. Let him out, please!" But Satan was unmoved, and the gates remained closed. The men did not know what else to do.

Finally, Joe's own dear mother went and stood outside the terrible gates. She did not bang or beseech or beg. Amazingly, she did not even ask for her son's release. Quietly and with determined voice, she simply said to Satan: "Let me in." Immediately the great doors swung open to admit her. "For love," Chesterton wrote, "goes down through the gates of hell, and there redeems the dead."[1]

Chesterton's parable would not have made much sense to me had I not walked with refugees these past twenty-five years. I started out not like Joe's mother, but rather, much more like Joe's buddies, thinking I could rescue the refugees from their hellish situations in the camps. I am now convinced that wisdom lies in simply being with them wherever they are. I came to this understanding rather slowly, and not without difficulty.

The six weeks that Nhia Bee's family spent at our motherhouse opened my eyes to a larger world, one that I was now eager to explore. And so I made arrangements through the friend of a friend to set off for Thailand for a year's immersion in a refugee camp.

When I first set out, I might as well have been Indiana Jones. Each day was sheer adventure. I'd never been out of the United States before, and now here I was flying off on my own to Bangkok. As I said earlier, my initial calling to this ministry had been through a dream in which it was quite clear that the refugees would be teaching me many things, above all "a new way of loving," but I'm afraid I lost sight of that humble perspective shortly after the wheels of the nearly empty 747 lifted off from the runway at the San Francisco Airport.

Besides the crew, the charter plane carried only ten passengers, all headed for work in refugee camps. The plane was heading to Thailand in order to pick up a full load of Southeast Asian refugees destined for permanent resettlement in the United States. In the company of nine seasoned refugee workers, I managed to transform myself, within the space of a twenty-two hour flight, into a grand emissary of mercy, an agent of God who would do great things, able to leap tall oceans in a single bound, sent to rescue beleaguered exiles.

I was overjoyed to be on my way. Never mind that I didn't care for rice (or camping, for that matter), spoke no foreign language, knew next to nothing about the refugee camps, had only a six-week visa (though I planned to stay a year), and had absolutely no idea where I would be working. In my pocket I carried the address of a convent in Bangkok, along with a written promise from one of the Sisters there that yes, certainly, she could find some way for me to work in a refugee camp somewhere in Thailand. Talk about unprepared! Yet I was incredibly happy and calm, confident that everything would fall into place. I slept peacefully for ten of those twenty-two hours and arrived in Bangkok alert and refreshed.

The year was 1981. The US hostages in Iran had just been freed. Ronald Reagan's elevation to the Oval Office, like a Hollywood script, was playing out before crowds who wanted to forget about domestic inflation, defeat in Vietnam, and humiliation in Tehran. Americans were yearning for old-fashioned, feel-good, flag-waving patriotism. But all was not well in the world. Partly as a humanitarian response to the televised anguish of the "boat people," partly to assuage our own national conscience about the war that had ended so badly—but mostly to address the political sensitivities of the United States' remaining allies in Southeast Asia—Congress had decided to allow tens of thousands of refugees into the United States from camps throughout the region. I, as a refugee camp worker, would be one small player in this brave new exodus.

Bangkok's Don Muang airport was, in those days, surrounded by rice paddies and patches of thick green vegetation spliced by dirt roads and transportation *klongs* (canals). Palm trees lined the runway. I stepped down from the plane onto a liquid-looking tarmac that shimmered with equatorial heat and walked into the terminal, where slow-moving, smiling immigration officers and customs inspectors greeted me and waved me through. So far, so good. One of my fellow passengers kindly offered me a lift into Bangkok in the van of her relief organization.

On that initial eighteen-mile ride into Bangkok, I nearly overdosed on the dizzying meld of unfamiliar sights and sounds and smells. We sped along on a fairly modern freeway, just inches away from women in sarongs and straw hats who were bent double, sweeping the roadside with short-handled brooms. We passed thatched houses on stilts above the narrow brown klongs. Closer to the city we saw huge construction projects underway, with barefoot men and women clambering up and down rickety high scaffolds made from bamboo lashed together with vines of some sort.

As we neared Bangkok, the traffic slowed and thickened and then clogged: cars, vans, and buses belching black fumes; open-air three-wheeled *samlors* (taxis), motorcyclists, and bicycle riders dodging in and out; not to mention the occasional elephant plodding along, prodded by a mahout astride its thick neck. Traffic moved on the left, British style, but without lanes or discernible traffic regulations. Swirls of chaotic movement vied for the same space, accompanied by the honking of horns and the dashing of pedestrians across the streets wherever the noisy churning clotted enough to allow it.

There was literally too much for my Western eyes to see. Sidewalks crammed with vendors walking along with heavy baskets slung from poles over their shoulders. Fruit stands, beggars, shops, and shrines. Incense from the street-side altars mixing strangely with the sizzling smell of who-knows-what from hidden kitchens. Buddhist monks in yellow robes walking beside men in finely-tailored business suits. Pictures of Levi's jeans and Fanta cola on giant billboards looming over families who squatted on the sidewalks, cooking their breakfasts on tiny charcoal fires. My brain was on sensory overload by the time the van dropped me off at my destination, a walled convent compound on Bangkok's Ploenchit road.

The community of Sisters there—native Thai nuns as well as missionaries from France, the Netherlands, and the United States—were exceedingly gracious to me. My guest room had open latticework on two sides, and when the monsoon rains came that first night, I realized why. The hot winds could blow freely through the room without knocking the walls down. This fascinated me, as did the lightning and tremendous thunderclaps. The next morning I learned that several tiles from the spot directly over my bed had been dislodged by a lightning bolt that struck the roof. That just added to my general excitement. I felt close to the Earth, close to the life pulsing through the place.

I spent one week in Bangkok acclimating to the weather and food and making arrangements with the Catholic Office for Emergency Relief and Refugees for my assignment. Then I rode twelve hours north-by-northeast on a train to the village of Nong Khai, the location of the refugee camp where I began teaching English.

During the ensuing months, as I worked side-by-side with the Lao refugees who lived within the barbed-wire enclosure of that dusty, forgotten corner of the Earth, those images of myself as Super-nun wilted completely.

The Vietnam War had ended six years earlier, but its proxy war in neighboring Laos was still simmering. Organized resistance to the Communist government by the Hmong and other groups inside Laos collapsed in 1975 with the withdrawal of American funding and advisers, and many thousands of Lao people were arrested and held in "seminars," a euphemism for forced labor camps. They were imprisoned and "reeducated," as one Lao refugee explained it to me, "until our thinking would be right." When these internees escaped or were released, some joined secret guerilla resistance groups; thousands of others looked for ways to escape from the country. They became refugees.

These refugees, I soon learned, were held in local jails after they had crossed the Mekong River and landed on the Thai side of the border. After being interrogated, they were processed into the camp. Their living quarters were eighteen inches of space per person on a six-foot deep bamboo shelf in long, thatched barracks, with a flimsy fabric curtain hung to separate the compartments. A family of four, for example, lived on a platform six feet square. It was raised a few inches above the dirt ground to provide some protection from scorpions and snakes, of which there were plenty. Water was strictly rationed. A family of seven received three gallons in the morning, and three more in the evening. This had to suffice for cooking, drinking, bathing, and cleaning. Thai guards controlled the camp, and refugees needed special permits to go out even briefly. The United Nations had an office inside the camp, but their workers were largely powerless to enforce any standards except those sanctioned by the Thai government. A few non-governmental organizations were allowed to function inside the camp, running the camp hospital (a makeshift clinic in a narrow wooden barrack) and helping out in the schools.

I settled into a routine, month after month, of hypnotic sameness. The heat, the dust, the pervasive poverty, the unchanging pattern of the refugees' confined, artificial existence, all forged a strange sense of near-normalcy to the situation. Occasionally, however, I witnessed things that shook me deeply. A three-year-old girl singing to herself while she played with her newfound toy: a dead rat on a string. Newlyweds who had nothing to serve to their wedding guests but watermelon seeds (until the local Sisters saved the day with a bottle of whiskey). The drowning death of a refugee child in one of the camp ponds: "We couldn't have prevented it," the grieving parents explained. "That pond is haunted."

My adult students were, compared to most of the American teens I had taught, positively zealous in their pursuit of learning. In the Lao culture, teachers are revered; accordingly, the refugees treated me like near-royalty. They were accustomed only to rote learning. Teacher says a sentence; students repeat it in unison. I, however, taught American-style. We engaged in spontaneous conversations, we did role plays, we invented grammar games; we read short stories and then discussed them. In their eyes, I was the world's most creative teacher. They greeted my simplest lesson plans with rapt attention. No one was ever absent. One morning Sourasith came to class shivering, sweating, and flushed. I asked if he was sick. "Oh yes, I have malaria; but I didn't want to miss class!"

Over time I learned their stories. A twenty-five-year-old named Viengthong told of spending many years in "seminar." He described being locked into a room with seventy other men. For two years and eight months, he was never allowed out of that room. He never had a bath. He never had a change of clothing. Thirty-seven of his companions died. The room had one small window. When it rained, everyone crowded near it to catch some of the water trickling in so that they could wash. At one point several prisoners who had been Viengthong's friends escaped. As punishment, the guards bound Viengthong's legs to a wooden board for six months, leaving him unable to move.

When he was finally released, his legs remained useless for another two months. He dreamed only of crossing the Mekong to freedom. As soon as he was strong enough to walk and swim, he escaped to Thailand. Three of his brothers and sisters had fled earlier, but he had no idea where they were—elsewhere in Thailand? in America? France? Australia? Now he was alone in Nong Khai, confined to a refugee camp ringed by guard towers and barbed wire, but happy to be alive.

There was great excitement in Nong Khai the morning that a baby elephant swam across the Mekong from the Lao side to the Thai side. Villagers quickly corralled it. The joke then circulated that, when the police interviewed it, the elephant claimed to have escaped because it didn't want to live under a Communist government.

To many of the refugees, it wasn't a joke. Some in the camp were members of the Lao Freedom Fighters, a collection of resistance groups that operated nineteen semi-secret guerilla encampments along the border. Each group answered to a different leader. The groups worked independently, but all had the same goal of harassing and ambushing military troops inside Laos. Kham Oui, one of my adult students, often bragged of the Freedom Fighters' exploits. At his repeated urging, I agreed one day to visit some of the guerrilla sites. The trip was hastily and quietly arranged, as these encampments were off-limits to foreigners.

Kham Oui and I climbed into a battered pickup truck, which then sped along the road that roughly parallels the Mekong. Every hour or so, the truck veered off the road and stopped beneath a tangle of trees.

The driver jumped out and motioned for us to follow him into the forest. Soon a young soldier would meet us and take us into the camp.
An honor guard of sorts—a ragtag lineup of twenty men and three
women—had been assembled to greet us at the first camp. They offered us flowers. They stood at attention in the heat, not moving (even
though biting red ants swarmed over their sandaled feet) while the of-
ficer-in-charge gave a welcoming speech. I then spoke, using Kham
Oui as my interpreter, with two teenagers who said they'd been fighting for five years. "Yes, I've killed many enemy soldiers," said one in
response to my question.

In another such camp there were groups of young men whose
black hair hung far below their shoulders. They had vowed never to
cut it, they told me, until Laos was once again a free country. The
next camp, called Hui Suam, was ringed by bunkers fortified with
sandbags. About fifty soldiers lounged about, but their uniforms were
tattered, and their thatched huts in disrepair. One hundred of their
compatriots, I was told, were across the river, fighting inside Laos.
The leader disclosed that he had recently lost sixty men in fierce fighting. Of course, it was impossible to verify their stories, though it was
clear that these people had made a serious commitment to the resistance effort.

At Ban Pheng, another camp, I met a twelve-year-old boy guarding the place with a rifle. I saw other children sick with "forest fever"
(malaria). I talked with a woman who commanded a fighting force of
thirty women. Now and then during my year in Nong Khai, I read reports in the Bangkok *Post* of military skirmishes on the Lao side of the
river. One such article corroborated the verbal description given by
one of the refugees that his guerrilla unit had blown up an ammunition depot inside Laos. The sad fact, however, was that these soldiers
were impossibly outnumbered and ill-equipped to tackle the Vietnamese who occupied their homeland. For the Lao Freedom Fighters, it
would be a long, terribly costly, and ultimately fruitless struggle.

During my year in the camp I witnessed numerous examples of corruption. One was particularly galling, since it involved adults stealing from refugee children. The German Red Cross announced that it would be delivering forty large crates of school supplies to the elementary school in Nong Khai camp. The whole student body assembled at 9:00 in the morning in the open courtyard. Under a blistering sun they stood in formation for three hours until the representatives finally arrived. Then they stood through tedious official speeches. All the while the students eyed the piles of cartons in front of them. The German delegate then opened one box, ceremoniously handed pencils and notebooks to exactly three students while getting his picture taken, and drove off waving from his air-conditioned van. The refugee camp commander, a burly Thai man who never smiled, stepped up and barked an order to his aides as soon as the visitor had disappeared: "Put half the crates into my van."

He dismissed the assembly and drove off in a cloud of dust to sell his stolen goods for personal profit. I was appalled, then indignant, then outraged. The Lao teachers, for their part, tried to calm me down. "Are you surprised? This happens all the time. We must be grateful for what we receive, not upset by what never reaches us." They went on to explain, "Why do you think we are always hungry? It's because two-thirds of the rice rations from the UN 'disappears' before distribution." This was my introduction to the daily indignities endured by the refugee poor.

Their maddening passivity, however, only fueled my fury. That night I told the Sisters that I intended to write an exposé of the incident for the local newspaper. Seriously alarmed, they begged me to reconsider. "At the very least, you will be expelled from the camp and your visa revoked. More likely, you will be killed. We would find your body floating in the Mekong. How would that help the refugees? Write the story if you wish," they advised me, "but not until the year is over and you are back home in the States."

Just before my year there ended, Nong Khai camp was shut down by the Thai government, and all its inhabitants bused a full day's drive to an "austerity camp" at Nakhon Phanom, in a more barren sector of northeast Thailand. For the refugees, it must have seemed the very end of the earth. The reason for the move? Some policy-makers in Bangkok had decided that Nong Khai camp was too luxurious—that it might be attracting people out of Laos, especially since (after years of waiting) some of the Nong Khai refugees were now being considered for resettlement in France, Australia, or America. To erase any such incentive for further refugee inflows, the Thai government planned to raze Nong Khai camp. The new camp, Nakhon Phanom, would be closed: no outsiders permitted. Food and water would be rationed much more tightly. There would be few health or educational services inside. And most discouraging of all, the refugees would not be eligible to interview for the possibility of permanent resettlement in the West. The austerity-camp policy thus narrowed their future to a forced choice: either stay inside the refugee camp forever, or repatriate (that is, return voluntarily) to Laos. Watching those buses carry my refugee friends off to Nakhon Phanom was one of the bleakest hours of my life.

It made my coming home all the harder. The refugees I'd grown so close to were now in the austerity camp. They didn't have enough to eat. They didn't ever expect to be released or resettled elsewhere. They were cut off from the outside world. Meanwhile, I was back in the United States, where my friends were eager to celebrate my homecoming and take me out to dinner to hear all about my adventures. Sitting in a restaurant, facing a full plate of food, I would see only the refugees' meager rations. I knew that the amount on my plate could feed an entire family. The food stuck in my throat. Hiking with friends in the California foothills, surrounded by the beauty of open fields and wildflowers, I would visualize the confinement of the refugees who had no freedom of movement, their days circumscribed by double rows of barbed wire fencing. My choice to spend ten dollars seeing a movie with a friend weighed on me; that money, if sent instead to the camp, could have purchased medicine for Somchai's sick child.

A pervasive sadness settled over me. Sure, my friends enjoyed the stories about strange things I had eaten (I enjoyed recounting them), but very few really wanted to hear me talk about the refugees' anguished lives. Perhaps they thought I exaggerated. Maybe they didn't want to know about problems halfway around the world. Certainly the stories I told were out of place in suburban America, where the word *camping* conjures summer vacations, not misery upon misery.

Most of all, I was hopelessly inept in the telling. The pain I felt because of my involvement in the lives of the refugees lay heavy and unspoken within me, like a wounded animal. I had no clue how to communicate it. What good were words, anyway? My friends had not been where I'd been, had not seen what I'd seen. How could I expect them to feel what I was feeling? Was there any chance that this world could overlap with their world—my former world—in any comprehensible way? Could I straddle both, or did I need to choose?

At the time, I had never heard the words *reverse culture shock*. Not really knowing what I was going through, I pushed aside my sadness and plunged into working for a graduate degree in social work at UC Berkeley, the degree that would position me to do refugee resettlement work stateside. By day, I pretended to care about my studies. I participated in classes, buried myself in the library stacks, wrote papers. By night, however, I painstakingly deciphered the letters that were arriving regularly from the austerity camp. With the help of my Lao dictionary, the words slowly untangled themselves from their foreign script and tumbled into troubled coherence on my desk:

> *Please, Sister, in your prayer ask God to bless my family, to let me be successful in my hope for resettlement. If I fail this time, how can I endure further in this camp without any hope and no more chance? This makes me thoughtful and sad. I am afraid I will be sick some day.*
>
> *—Khamphiou*

Sister, last night I dreamed you came back to the camp in a helicopter and rescued my family and me. I woke up happy, but it was not true.

—Syda

Sister, my life is hard now in this austerity camp. But I dug a well for my neighbor, and I think the God will remember this one good thing I have done in my life.

—Niraphay

Their correspondence piled up on my desk, making my academic work seem less and less relevant. I did what I could, answering their letters, enclosing money orders whenever I received a donation from a friend, letting the refugees know that they had not been forgotten. All the while my own survivor's guilt mounted. Of what possible use was a term paper when my friends were suffering? Why was I wasting time on this campus reading about the history of social work when I could be doing something practical to help the refugees?

I began reading the Gospels differently. The cure of the paralytic at the pool of Bethsaida (chapter 5 of John's Gospel) rewrote itself into my prayer journal:

Now in Thailand by Nakorn Phanom there is a place with the name Napho Camp. Inside its barbed wire enclosure 22,000 refugees lay paralyzed, without freedom, barely surviving—waiting for the slightest movement in the web of international policies that bind them. There were many who had been held captive there with their families for years and years. Jesus, who knew they had been stuck there for a long time, said to them, "Do you want to be freed?" "Sir," the refugees answered, "We do not have anyone to sponsor us even if the situation should change . . . "

My agitation increased. I stopped getting together with friends. I considered returning to Thailand to live inside the austerity camp with the refugees. Even today, I recognize that there is value simply in accompanying exiles, in choosing to remain with them. At the time the idea appealed to me strongly, but I knew that the Thai government now forbade the presence of foreigners inside the camp. Not even teachers or nurses were allowed in; I could never hope to gain access to live among the refugees now.

And what, precisely, could I do for them, anyway? What were my options? Being a nun with a vow of poverty, I had no personal income at my disposal. Maybe if I left the convent and got a good job somewhere, I could send the money to the austerity camp. This thought was quite seductive, appealing as it did to my none-too-subliminal savior complex: *If God could not be roused to rescue the refugees, perhaps I could save them myself.* Prayer was becoming difficult. When I did pray, it was more like sparring. For some time I gave it up entirely. I was angry with God. There was no end to the suffering of the refugees. Didn't God care?

On my annual prayer retreat, I wrote an open letter to God, spilling forth my feelings:

Yahweh,

Do you see these tears? Have you read any of these letters from the austerity camp? Can you see Bounchanh and his wife and children? He writes that his heart is broken, but that he still finds some peace because he truly believes you will some day "help him to get out of this . . ." I cried—no, I broke down and sobbed—when I read those words. Then I felt like screaming, "No, it's not true! God won't rescue the poor man." Oh, sure, I know that the Scriptures are full of such promises, but they seem empty now, all of them.

When has the poor man ever really been saved? (And I don't mean after death; that hardly seems to count.) Shall I write to Bounchanh and tell him that it's all been a terrible lie? He is one of the few Christians in the camp, and he looks to me for support and encouragement in his faith. Well, he'd surely be scandalized if I shared what I'm really feeling right now: there is no way out for him. The poor will always lose. No one cares about—or even knows about—the austerity camp. America isn't going to help the Lao people. You aren't going to help them, either. And I am powerless to help them.

But the faces are still here, God. I see them one by one. I know them by name. They are my students, and I am still their teacher. Their letters keep coming:

Sister, if you receive my letter, please answer and give some opinion that push my heart to be happy.

—Souksavanh

Sister, I was 20 years in the army, 6 years 2 months and 25 days as a prisoner of war in Laos, and now how long will I be in this refugee camp?

—Komsensee

Sister, don't let me down about the sponsor. I and my family depend on you.

—Bounchanh

Teachers are revered by the Lao people. These refugees now look to me, their former teacher, and write to me with utter candor. They pin their hopes on me. But what can I do in response? Nothing! I'm not an ambassador; I don't have political connections. I'm not good at crusading. I was born to lead a quiet life. You called me and led me to identify with the poor, and I gladly followed; but now look what's happened! All these refugees have turned to me—but I don't even have an independent salary to share with them. Besides that, my friends tell me I've changed, and they no longer know how to connect with me. I feel unspeakably sad.

You know very well I'm angry with you, God. Restless. Unable to pray. Why don't you break down the dividing wall that keeps us apart? I don't feel any initiative from you, any outreach. All I feel is this awful lump of smoldering anger. And guilt, paralyzing guilt. How am I to enjoy the luxuries here—the ample food, the swimming pool, our carpeted and cushioned lifestyle? None of it is bad, but I can't relax and "go with it" anymore. Being home is not working well for me.

Lately, I've tried admitting the pain of it, telling friends little by little. But where are you, God? Are You the comforter of the afflicted? Refuge of the poor? God-who-has-always-been-with-me? Or are you a God who sees but does nothing? God who allows sickness when there is no money for medicine. God who speaks of love but lets cruelty reign. God who extols gentleness only to watch it be crushed behind barbed wire. God who listens to the prayers of rich Christians all over the globe but does not change their hearts. God in whose name wars are waged. God who remains silent in the midst of suffering. God who sidesteps all these questions by pointing to the cross.

Which God are you? And why don't you answer these tears? I have always wanted to love you.

God chose not to respond on my timeline. Nevertheless, the act of venting provided me some relief, and so I plowed back into academia with anger simmering on the back burner. God and I were now at a stand-off.

Then one day I experienced something like a waking dream. I was not praying, but merely sitting in a garden near the university, mulling over the mess in which I felt so mired. Without intending to, I suddenly found myself in dialog with the God whom I'd shunted aside for so many weeks.

Suppose you had a brother whom you loved, I said to God. Suppose your father lavished abundant gifts on you, but gave nothing to your brother. In fact, he locked him out in the backyard and ignored him, leaving only a small bowl of scraps for him to eat once each day. How long could you continue to enjoy all of your own comforts and privileges inside the house? How long could you abide "praying for your brother" from a distance? How long before you would begin to resent this father who supposedly loves all his children, especially the poor?

And if you spent some time outside in that empty yard with your brother and grew very close to him and felt his anguish at not being able to feed and clothe his own children, and saw that—despite the mistreatment—he still loved his father and asked imploringly, 'What did I ever do to offend our father, that he should treat me this way?'

After all that, would you want to meet your father again face-to-face inside your comfortable house? Wouldn't you be afraid that you would hate him?

And much to my surprise, God replied:

> *You know that's not how it is, Marilyn, though I understand why you feel this way. I have many children. Some of them locked your brother out of the house. My heart is out there with him, but I've left people free. They do with me as they please. You see, love can't force anything. I'm as powerless, really, as a quadriplegic. They surround me with linen and candles, with solemn processions and profusions of flowers, and they deluge me with their prayers. But oddly enough, only a few of them really take notice of their brothers and sisters. It breaks my heart, too.*
>
> *I'm glad you've noticed them. Go ahead; be angry, but please don't hate me. I am with you in this, more than you could ever realize. And I am with your brothers and sisters in the camps, too, even as I am blamed for the burdens they now bear. Come now, let your tears flow. See, I am weeping with you.*

Our stand-off ended right then and there, as God and I wept together in that Berkeley garden. Since that moment, I have understood God differently. No matter what the theologians may say to the contrary, I know that God is *not* All-Powerful, at least not as most of us understand power. Why not? Because those who love never exert control over others.[2] Because loving makes us utterly vulnerable, as C.S. Lewis described in his book *The Four Loves*:

> To love at all is to become vulnerable. Love anything and your heart will certainly be wrung and possibly broken. If you want to make sure of keeping it intact, you must

give your heart to no one, not even to an animal. Wrap it carefully round with hobbies and little luxuries; avoid all entanglements; lock it up safely in the casket or coffin of your selfishness. But in that casket-safe, dark, motionless, airless space, it will change. It will not be broken; it will become unbreakable, impenetrable, irredeemable. The alternative to tragedy, or at least to the risk of tragedy, is damnation. The only place outside Heaven where you can be perfectly safe from all the dangers and perturbations of love is Hell.[3]

Chesterton was right. Love wants to be with the beloved. Love can't fix things, but love always knocks and comes right in to be with the beloved in the midst of their suffering, even to the depths of hell. Love does not isolate or insulate; love chooses to *be with*. Love does not coerce; it can only invite. God waits: "Here I stand, knocking at the door. If anyone hears me calling and opens the door, I will enter the house and sup with her, and she with me" (Rv 3:20).

Despite our persistent and stubborn expectations to the contrary, God never promises to take away our pain, but rather pledges to remain close to us in the midst of it. The prophets invite us to "call his name Emmanuel, which means, God With Us" (Is 7:14). We have God's word on it: "Behold, I am with you always, until the end of the age" (Mt 28:20).

On this pledge, everything depends.

A $\mathscr{K}$NOCK ON THE $\mathscr{D}$OOR

Icy rain pelted the windows of our inner-city convent one Friday evening as eight of us were enjoying dinner together in the dining room, happy to be indoors. The front doorbell unexpectedly buzzed. I turned in my chair, but no one else budged. Being new to that place (I had just arrived on the East Coast for an internship that would complete my UC Berkeley studies) and also being the youngest, I jumped up and ran down the long hallway to answer the door. Outside, looking miserable in the wintry, rain-slicked grayness, stood a shivering young man roughly the age of one of my younger brothers.

"Excuse me, ma'am," he began hesitantly, "I wonder if I could get a bite to eat?"

"Sure," I answered, giving him the standard reply. "Just go around the corner to the priests' rectory and they will take care of you."

"I already tried that," he mumbled, staring at his shoes. "They told me to come back on Monday between nine and five."

"Well, in that case," I said, inwardly seething at the thought that a church would turn away a hungry person for three days, "you are most welcome to eat here."

I ushered him in, leading him past the inner set of doors, carefully locking them behind us, and then back through the dark hall that led into the kitchen, across from the dining room. When the stranger removed his coat and hat, I saw how his thick brown hair stuck wetly at all angles. His worn shirt smelled of damp wool from the cold drizzle that had seeped under his collar. He perched self-consciously on the edge of his chair while I heated up a bowl of soup and fixed coffee along with a few sandwiches. We sat opposite each other for twenty or thirty minutes while he ate. Soft-spoken and with intelligent eyes, he gave the impression of being well-educated but, for the moment at least, without means. I wanted to respect his privacy, so we talked about ordinary things while he finished every last crumb. I offered to let him take a hot shower in the back room. He declined, insisting that he'd already caused enough trouble. Then, thanking me profusely, he allowed me to show him out into the night.

Securing the double sets of doors behind me once again, I returned to the dining room, only to be confronted by stony glares from everyone around the table. Finally, one of the nuns (the gentlest in that entire community) broke the hostile silence:

"Just what was that all about? You endangered all our lives when you let that man in here. For all we know, he could have been an axe-murderer! What were you thinking?"

It didn't seem the right moment to mention that I'd actually been thinking how wonderful it is that God often comes to us in the form of a stranger.

Instead, I defended my action. I described how the young man had been rebuffed at the rectory and then asked them, rhetorically, "Well, what was I supposed to do? Turn him away at the door?"

"Yes!" "Exactly!" "Of course!" they retorted, their voices tight with anger.

Incredulous, I stood my ground, "But how could I turn away a hungry person from our door?"

The logic of their reply stopped me cold: "If you'd never gone to the door in the first place, you wouldn't have had to turn him away."

If not A, then not B. Simple. Avoid encountering strangers and you will never have to deal with them. Don't ever put yourself in a situation where strangers might make demands on you or your lifestyle. Don't ever open the door. Don't make eye contact. Don't let strangers' needs impinge on your life.

Of course, common sense told me that they were right. I later learned that those nuns had good reason for their reaction. Several convents in the neighborhood had recently been broken into, and in one case a nun had been raped. No wonder they were angry at me, the naïve newcomer on the block, stupidly putting them all at risk. Nevertheless, this incident profoundly affected the course of my own life. It delineated for me the choice between common sense and gospel invitation. I decided then and there, on that drizzly winter night, never again to live behind barriers that would separate me from the poor. I resolved to put myself precisely in places where I could open doors to strangers, even in a world full of danger. My life's purpose crystallized, from that point forward, into simply the "welcoming of strangers." I shall always be deeply grateful to those Sisters for providing the jolt that so clearly focused my life.

A little more than a year before, I was unknowingly prepared for my rainy night epiphany. One day during my first trip to Thailand, Sr. Mary Eduouard had asked me a strange question. She, the resident elder in our little convent on the bank of the Mekong River, had turned to me casually as we were sharing a meal together, using our fingers to pull steamed sticky rice from a common basket, rolling it into little balls between our fingers and dipping them into fish sauce.

"I have heard," she began politely, "that in America, it is *one person, one room; one person, one plate*. Is that true?"

Supposing this to be a complimentary reference to America's high standard of living, I smiled and nodded, "Yes, it is for the most part true."

Eduouard's questioning gaze faded to puzzlement as she weighed the cultural poverty of my response. Slowly shaking her head, she sighed aloud, "Aaah, but why would *anyone* want to live like *that*?"

After my year of living in a refugee camp, I knew I couldn't—and indeed didn't want to—isolate myself any longer from persons in need. I was, of course, familiar with the Scriptures and had always loved the image of Jesus described in the final book of the Christian Scriptures: "Behold, I stand at the door and knock. If anyone hears my voice and opens the door, I will enter his house and dine with him, and he with me" (Rv 3:20). But until that rainy winter night at our convent, I suppose I'd always spiritualized the passage: God knocks on my heart and my receptivity in turn leads to communion with the Divine. Now, however, the passage took on a literal, street-level meaning. Looking at the problem of the stranger, both in Thailand and back in the United States, I began to see that if I were to continue to work with refugees, it could not be merely a ministering to them, as it had been initially, but a welcoming of the God who comes to meet me in them. Through these strangers, sometimes distressing, sometimes achingly beautiful, sometimes scary, God was knocking at the door. Whether it was a Hmong refugee or an urban homeless man, no matter. God was knocking.

Twenty years after the incident with the homeless man, I was talking with a group of Sudanese refugees whom my co-workers at Catholic Charities were resettling in San Jose, California. Upon their arrival at the airport, we had greeted the new arrivals warmly, given them "welcome packs"—backpacks that volunteers had donated and stuffed with useful items for newcomers—and placed the refugees into secure housing. A month later I asked the refugees to think back on their first few weeks in America. "What were your initial impressions of the

United States? What surprised you the most?" I had witnessed first-hand the devastation caused by Sudan's long civil war and the subsequent deprivation these young adults had endured for nearly a dozen years in the barren refugee camps of northeast Africa. So I expected these newcomers to say that they were dazzled by the tall buildings, the freeways, the computers, and other high-tech marvels that populate our American landscape. Or that they appreciated having abundant food for the first time in their lives, real beds to sleep in, and books to read. Instead, eighteen-year-old Atem piped up immediately, grinning widely, eyes brimming with happiness:

"What surprised me most? I will tell you! Never in my life could I have imagined that someone would *welcome me* like this!"

Welcome is something that refugees don't often experience. As targets either of war or persecution or both, they leave their home countries because they are no longer welcome. Their lives are not safe. They flee to neighboring lands, where a cordial reception is extremely unlikely. Most refugees find themselves blocked at national borders, summarily turned back by immigration officers, or arrested in the new country for lack of proper visas and documentation.

Sometimes, when a particular refugee flow is massive enough, the world briefly takes notice and the United Nations High Commissioner for Refugees (UNHCR) receives permission from the receiving country to erect a camp for the refugees' temporary safety. Usually this occurs in developing countries already struggling with significant problems of their own. Thus, in the 1990s the tiny country of Malawi—with a population of only eight million—opened its borders to one million refugees escaping from the civil war in neighboring Mozambique, and Iran allowed several million Afghanis to take shelter within its rugged eastern border. Kenya, having the misfortune to be surrounded by refugee-producing countries, has long tolerated refugee camps on three of its borders.

The presence of refugees in any country is viewed by the host government, with good reason, as destabilizing. In Africa, for example, large refugee populations have damaged the fragile ecosystems in which they settle. As the refugees cut down trees for fuel and tap into scarce reserves of water, animosity increases among the local inhabitants who understandably resent the intrusion of tens of thousands of foreigners onto their land. To make matters worse, refugee camp populations often include former combatants and nearly always attract rebel recruiters crossing into the camps to recruit young men back into the fighting. Refugees soon grow accustomed to being treated as unwelcome burdens.

It is our practice at Catholic Charities in San Jose to bring a welcome sign to the airport whenever we meet refugees arriving from camps overseas. Each sign has the refugee's name on it and, when possible, a welcome message written in the refugee's own language. This is not so the refugees will be able to find us, as if they were business travelers searching the crowd for a sign held by a waiting limo driver. Rather, it's because we want the new arrivals' first moments in America to be positive.

The refugees are generally the last persons to disembark from the airplane. Their faces, showing weariness imbedded by years of suffering and loss, peer out anxiously beyond the jetway into the boarding area of the airport:

What awaits us at the end of this ramp? How will we manage without knowing the language? Will we have the strength to start over in a strange new place? What if no one is here to show us what to do next?

One Nigerian refugee family, overcome by the sight of our small welcome party waving and holding aloft a poster bearing their names, burst into tears. The father of the family later explained,

> We didn't really have any idea what to expect, but I had supposed that we would be confronted in the airport by military personnel who would yell at us: "You! Follow me!" It was entirely beyond my thinking that Americans would be friendly and greeting us and treating us with respect.

When the U.S. military left Vietnam in 1975, they left behind thousands of offspring, children who were half-American, half-Vietnamese and who came to be known as "Amerasians"—*bui doi* in Vietnamese, roughly translatable as "the dust of life." Their blue eyes, brown hair, or freckles marked them for ridicule in school, children of the enemy, doubly unwanted in a society that places great value on racial purity.

After the war ended, many Vietnamese mothers viewed these children as albatrosses identifying themselves as enemy collaborators, so they abandoned them to the streets. Many years later, Congress passed the Amerasian Homecoming Act, authorizing permanent resettlement in the United States for all of the Vietnamese Amerasians. From 1990–1995 I was involved in the domestic resettling of the Amerasians, who were by that time young adults. Their faces looked very American but they spoke little English.

One tall, freckle-faced young Amerasian named Yen (pronounced very much like the English word "in") laughed as he told me how, during his first few weeks in America, his sponsor often walked him to various homes in their neighborhood, to help him make new acquaintances. Yen was amazed and delighted, day after day, by identical heartwarming experiences. He and his sponsor would ring a new doorbell, and within a minute the door would open to a smiling face that greeted him exuberantly, "Come in!" He naturally heard it as "Come, Yen!" Mystified, he finally asked his sponsor, "How do all these people know my name?"

We all want to live where somebody knows us. We want to be welcomed in and made to feel at home. God has a way of doing exactly that. In the Hebrew scriptures, the prophet Isaiah recounts God's promises in lovely images: "I have called you by name: you are mine"; "Upon the palms of my hands I have written your name" (Is 43:1; 49:16).

What does it mean to know someone's name? In our fast-paced Western culture, it usually means nothing more than words on a business card or the superficial ability to match a name with a face. But the biblical meaning of knowing someone's name goes much deeper. It literally means being in an intimate relationship with that person. Here lies the wonderful significance of the creation story in Genesis, chapter 2: God *names* the man and woman, and they in their turn *name* the animals and birds and creatures of the sea. We are meant to be in relationship with this God and with all of creation. In Genesis 32, Jacob wrestles all night with an angel (a stand-in for God) and in the morning cries out, "I will not let you go until you tell me your name!"

In the Hebrew scriptures we see that God is not too quick to hand out the divine name to everyone who asks. When Moses insists on knowing it, even to the point of repeatedly arguing with God, God's cagey response is "Tell the Israelites that YHWH sent me to you." Variously translated as "I am the One who is," or "I am who I am," or "I am the one who always is," YHWH remains a name that can never be fully grasped, but only understood, partially and tantalizingly, by those who experience God.

When my youngest brother was a third-grader, his religion class had been assigned to prepare posters for a church liturgy. I noticed that he was putting the finishing touches on a large sign that read Y-A-H-W-E-H, so I quizzed him to see if he knew what it meant. He looked up at me, still gripping his fat blue marking pen, and said, "I'm not sure. But I think it's some kind of a cheer." I have studied my share of theology courses, but to this day I still consider my brother's answer to be one of humankind's better descriptions of God.

Further on in the scriptures, there emerged from the Israelites' cumulative experience of God an abundance of names for the divine reality who still remains unknowable in full: Wonderful Counselor, Father, Comforter, Prince of Peace, Shepherd, Merciful One, Potter, Creator, Beloved. We are given repeated assurances that this God seeks our hearts' affection but also expects us in turn to show our love by caring for the widows, orphans, and aliens among us.

In the life and teaching of Jesus, this reality becomes very concrete. He welcomes everyone—innocent children and fishermen, tax collectors and lepers, sinners and prostitutes—into his presence. No need to have your life in order or your affairs tidy or your heart clean. Just "knock and the door will be opened" (Mt 7:7).

It's that simple. God stands ready to embrace us all, no questions asked. God promises not only to open the door whenever we knock, to welcome us in, give us a place at the table and dine with us, but also (and this should startle us!) to don an apron and serve us.

> Blessed are those servants whom the master finds vigilant on his arrival. Amen, I say to you, he will gird himself, have them recline at table, and proceed to wait on them. (Lk 12:37)

Surely this is staggeringly good news, such flagrantly prodigal behavior on God's part, sweeping aside all of our rigid rules for earning divine favor.

It isn't fair, of course, and the Pharisees (the most zealously religious persons of their era) were the first to notice and be upset. God flips upside down all our hard-fought expectations of worthiness. God's door is never locked, no matter who we are or what we've done. Anyone—everyone—can come in. Having experienced this unreserved, undeserved, flat-out welcome ourselves, we must grapple with the obvious consequence: How can we do anything less than offer this same unconditional welcome to others?

A good modern-day example of this kind of hospitality and "wide-awakeness" was Kenneth Unterer, the Bishop of Saginaw, Michigan, who until his death in 2004 took this stance of Jesus very much to heart. At his ordination as bishop he announced to the assembled congregation, "Hello, my name is Ken, and I'll be your waiter . . ." He understood that following Jesus meant a life of service. He made it practical, too, by selling the episcopal mansion and more or less living out of his car for many years, moving from parish to parish to be with the people. No wonder he was so beloved.

In the West, most of us live amid such abundance that even when we give away money or possessions, we still have more than enough.

This is not true for the poor. In refugee camps, there is never enough food. Usually the United Nations personnel distribute rations twice monthly, but each family's portion runs out a few days before the next allotment. On those days the refugees simply do not eat. When I visited a Somali refugee camp in Mombasa, Kenya, in 1992, I was aghast to discover that the Somali always cooked more than what they could eat each day, in order to have enough to share with visitors, on the off chance that someone might happen to stop by. Their nomadic roots compelled them to prepare to offer hospitality even when there was no sign of anyone approaching. It would have been unthinkable to cook just for one's *own* family. This meant, of course, that if no one stopped by (after all, how many people visit a refugee camp that is ringed by barbed wire and guarded by the military?), food would be wasted since no refrigeration was available; and always the families' rations would be gone faster than what the UN calculated, and the refugees would go without eating anything for several days.

My efficient American mind was annoyed: "This is crazy! Mete out your rations carefully! Don't waste a single grain of rice!" To this day, it still bothers me. Yet another part of me recognizes that this desert tradition in its own reckless way mirrors the prodigal generosity of God, who, without caring about consequences, throws open the door to all who desire to enter and be nourished. God's ways are never miserly, never measured. With God, we don't get what we come for; we always get more.

During World War II a remarkable network of hospitality opened up in France for Jews fleeing Nazi Germany. The married couple who started the movement, Pastor André Trocmé and his wife, Magda, did not set out to do anything heroic. Their faith led them simply to open their front door to anyone who knocked. In 1940 the first to knock was a Jewish woman seeking a place to hide, and they provided sanctuary. This stance of openness by Magda and her husband, maintained throughout the war despite increasingly serious personal risk, grew into an extensive, highly organized secret network for the protection and education of Jewish children. Throughout the war their village, Le Chambon, was the safest place in Europe for Jews. The entire population of the village cooperated in hiding over five thousand Jews—some for as long as four years—and smuggling many of them into Switzerland. With admirable understatement, one of the villagers later described his involvement:

> Things had to be done, and we happened to be there to do them. It was the most natural thing in the world to help these people.[1]

I beg to differ: It was not natural at all. These were dangerous, life-threatening choices made repeatedly over the span of five years. Yet, in what came to be known as a "conspiracy of goodness," the entire village kept their daring work completely secret. Not a single Jew was ever turned away, betrayed, or arrested in Le Chambon—though some of the organizers, including Pastor Trocmé, were themselves imprisoned by the Vichy government. Magda Trocmé and the other villagers continued their efforts despite knowing the dangers. Long after the war ended, Magda put it this way:

> I did not go around looking for people to help. But I never closed my door; I never refused to help someone who asked for something. This, I think, is my kind of religion. When things happen, not things that I plan, but things sent by God or by chance—when people come to my door—I feel responsible.[2]

This is my kind of religion, too.

$\mathcal{F}$OOD YOU KNOW $\mathcal{N}$OT OF

As a child I was a picky eater, often slipping much of my dinner onto a brother's plate when our parents weren't looking, or hiding offensive food under the overturned skin of a baked potato and then trying to look nonchalant while clearing the dishes to the kitchen. Some nights I sat close-mouthed at the dinner table until bedtime rather than eat the "greenies" (vegetables) on my plate. Truthfully, I have never completely outgrown this fussiness. So it was with considerable misgiving that my best friends assessed my decision to go to Thailand.

"You're doing *what?*" they objected. "You've never been out of the United States, you're afraid of spiders, and you don't even like rice!"

"Never mind," I assured them, dismissing their concerns. "I can learn."

Two weeks later I was on the night train from Bangkok to Nong Khai, riding twelve hours north by northeast into the unknown. The journey would take me from the teeming urban experience of Bangkok—where at least there had been a few American nuns to anchor my first week in Southeast Asia—to the extremes of the rural Thai countryside, where I knew no one. When the train chugged away from Bangkok's cavernous central station amid plumes of steam, screeching wheels, and unintelligible announcements from the loudspeakers, the sky was already dark. I relaxed and settled in for the night. After all, I could not possibly miss my destination. The village of Nong Khai, located on the southern bank of the Mekong River that formed Thailand's border with Laos, was quite literally the end of the line.

At dawn a red sun popped above the horizon, jolting me from sleep and drenching me in sudden daylight. I blinked a few times before the clickety-clacking train wheels reminded me where I was. Outside my compartment window the picturesque countryside was rushing by: clusters of thatched huts on stilts, water buffalo knee-deep in flooded rice fields, adults slowly riding bicycles on dirt paths, and soldiers holding machine guns. Machine guns? Now I was fully awake. Yes, every time the train slowed to pass through a village, there were soldiers standing on the wood-plank platforms with machine guns slung casually across their arms. Occasionally one or two would board the train for a few minutes to peer into the compartments, looking for what I did not know.

But I had more immediate things on my mind: I needed to find a bathroom. "*Hong ap nam?*" I inquired, guessing at the pronunciation indicated in my Lao dictionary and hoping it was close enough to Thai (I didn't have a Thai dictionary) for my fellow passengers to understand. Sure enough, a friendly gentleman pointed me toward a slim door at the end of the train. I slipped quickly inside and closed the door. Hmm. I saw nothing resembling a toilet, as there was only a string hanging along one wall and a round hole about three inches in diameter in the center of the floor, beneath which I could see the train tracks whizzing by. Oh well, make do. I aimed at the hole and did my thing, then emerged and returned nonchalantly to my compartment. Two hours later, as the train was pulling into Nong Khai, I walked past that end of the train again and saw, much to my chagrin, that the *hong ap nam* was the narrow door *opposite* the one I had used. Apparently I had relieved myself in the shower.

Properly humbled, I stepped off the train to greet the morning and my new home for the coming year. Sister Raphael, local superior of the small convent where I would be living, welcomed me with the gracious warmth that I soon discovered was typical of the Thai people. She escorted me to the convent, a two-story cinder-block building with chapel and dining area on the first floor and bedrooms on the upper floor. The kitchen, an open-air, charcoal-fire-on-the-ground affair, was outdoors. A profusion of lush tropical bushes, bamboo, flowers, and fruit trees formed a large garden in the rear.

By now it was nearly 9:00 a.m. The four resident Sisters had eaten long before my arrival. In tentative English aided by hand gestures, Raphael asked me if I was hungry, and I answered that, yes, I was quite hungry. This response sparked a flurry of activity. I was immediately seated at the table and given a very large bowl of rice. Rice for breakfast? In my ignorance about how the rest of the world eats, this was new to me. *Mai pen rai*, I reminded myself, practicing the handy Thai phrase for *Never mind*. Smiling, I thanked them. I could handle this.

I was feeling proud of myself until the next course arrived: a bowl full of frogs. Miniature frogs. Miniature *whole* frogs, their legs and arms splayed, staring woefully at me. I stared back even more woefully. From the way their skin glistened, flecked with bits of red pepper, I supposed that they'd been stir-fried in some sort of spicy sauce. The Sisters were all watching me expectantly; after all, I had foolishly told them I was hungry. OK. Though it was a tad harder to maintain my smile now, I took a slow breath and dug in.

I ate all the rice and three of the frogs, carefully depositing their bones on the edge of the bowl. Sister Mary Eduoard, the elder in the group, asked me in halting French why I was not eating the bones. The bones? Eating the bones? Not wanting to risk death-by-choking on my very first day in Nong Khai, but not wanting to offend Eduoard, I replied simply that it was not the American custom. This seemed puzzling to her, but much to my relief, she accepted it with a thoughtful nod. I had made it through my first meal in Nong Khai. I now felt that I was ready for anything.

My self-confidence proved premature.

A few days later Raphael took us all for an outing in the parish van. We bounced along a succession of dirt roads for several hours. I felt buoyantly happy, fascinated by the newness of all the sights and smells and sounds. The van stopped here and there. We clambered up a ladder to visit an old woman living in a bamboo hut built on stilts. We walked across rice paddies to bring medicine to a sick child. We skirted large, snuffling hogs to visit a family in a modest hut. Finally, the van pulled over to a roadside vendor who was barbecuing chicken, or rather, who was squatting alongside the already-well-barbecued chicken, for I could see that it was charred completely black. We all watched from the van while Raphael chatted with the man, apparently bargaining over a suitable price. *Too bad the meat is overdone*, I mused. *Mai pen rai; I can always remove the skin.*

As we watched, Raphael settled on a price with the vendor, who then began lifting the pieces of chicken onto a large palm leaf. To my horror, the "char" immediately flew off the chicken—not char at all, but solid swarms of black flies!

To grasp the terror that shot through me at the sight of those flies lifting off *en masse* from my lunch, you must appreciate the antiseptic environment in which I had been raised. My mother attributed nearly all deadly diseases, and many lesser afflictions as well, to the common housefly. Dysentery. Cholera. Schistosomiasis. Polio. African sleeping sickness. Multiple miseries we could neither pronounce nor comprehend, but which we wholeheartedly believed would overcome us if a fly ever touched our food. To ward off such a sorry end to our young lives, my mother, God bless her, remained ever vigilant. When a fly did manage to enter our suburban house—which happened all the time, of course, because we kids rarely remembered to close doors behind us—Mom would sound the alert.

"Fly in the house! Quick, there's a *fly* in the house!"

And we would bound to our battle stations. Contrary to what you might suppose, our family did not own a fly-swatter. That would have been unthinkable. Fly swatters were filthy, contaminated objects that we certainly couldn't have hanging around, not even in the garage. Instead, Mom wielded an old towel. Waving it like a toreador to a bull, she'd chase the fly from room to room until she swooshed it—being careful, of course, never to let the towel actually *touch* the fly—out the open door. Triumphant, Mom would return to the kitchen, her family once again safe.

Looking back on it now, I imagine that the flies may actually have enjoyed these sorties. Perhaps they passed on the genetic wisdom from fly-generation to fly-generation. Can't you hear the buzz among the teens? "Hey, stop by this house. See how long you can zip around before they get you. Don't worry; they'll never hurt you. But it's quite a rush dodging that giant towel!"

Science classes later confirmed the substance of the germ-lore Mom had drilled into us. You never knew for sure, but could easily guess, what kinds of disgusting offal those hideous little fly feet had dipped into before they stepped onto your plate. So it was with a sickly smile masking my trepidation that I accepted two pieces of non-charred chicken from the palm leaf in Raphael's outstretched hand. I examined my conscience. I decided I was ready to die, though I felt it would be a pity to have traveled so far and not have more time to be with the refugees. Slowly, bleakly, I ate the chicken. I had to admit, it was delicious. All the same, I did not join in the nuns' idle noontime chatter. My attention remained on the specter of death so far from home. Subsequent anxious hours passed without incident, however, and fear gradually loosened its grip on my imagination. Remarkably, I contracted neither plague nor fever, nor even a hint of intestinal distress. I'm still amazed.

Much of what I ate in Thailand remains a mystery to me even to this day. The nuns' English did not include many vocabulary words related to food, and my knowledge of the Thai language was negligible. When faced with an unrecognizable new item at a meal, I generally ventured at least a small portion. The staple was, of course, rice at every meal, but it was usually served with cooked greens or colorful sauces or bits of fish. One night the garnish for our rice was a thick, brown, strong-smelling paste, very bitter to the tongue.

I asked in my politest voice, "Excuse me, but what is this?"

The faces around the table scrunched up in concentration, obviously at a loss as to how to explain this substance or its origin. *Mai pen rai.* We went on to another topic. The next night as we sat at table a heavy thunderstorm passed overhead. When the rain ceased, the cicadas started chirping. Sister Raphael cocked her head and pointed outside while smiling at me: "Remember. Last night. Brown." I paled, realizing I had been the unwitting consumer of mashed crickets, another protein source for my continued good health.

Not all my food adventures were disheartening, of course. Thailand produces an extraordinary array of delicious tropical fruits. Though these items are now available widely in US markets, when I was growing up that was not the case. During my year in Thailand I was introduced each month to wondrous varieties of exotic fruit. Fuzzy red *rambutan*, a name I loved for the way it rolled off my tongue. Breadfruit, papaya, and star fruit. *Mangosteen*, a dark purple sphere very sweet and custardy inside. *Noi na*, a pale green, gnarly-skinned fruit, full of delicate juiciness. Thumb-sized bananas, much denser and more flavorful than any I'd ever tasted.[1] My favorite treats were mangos, which the Thai prefer to eat while green, dipping slices as crisp as apples into sugar and dried peppers.

Many Thai fruits are so aromatic that their fragrance literally perfumes the whole house. One, however, defies adequate description: the dreaded *durian*. No one is indifferent to durian; either you crave it or you run away from it gasping for breath. Its smell is so pungent that by law in some countries, you cannot carry it onto a bus or plane or other enclosed space. Durian's exterior consists of rows of prickly brown spikes—as if warning, *Do Not Touch*. To me, durian's odor is putrid. The mere thought of anyone eating durian is incomprehensible to me, though it is reputed to be exquisitely delicious. It's a claim I shall never be able to verify.

Aside from durian, I enjoyed all the Thai fruit and also grew to love rice. Since we ate rice three times a day, every day, this was a sensible Darwinian adaptation on my part. Not all Thai foods, however, were so readily integrated into my diet.

After each of the hot, muggy days teaching in the refugee camp, I showered (that is, doused myself with tepid water from a bucket), changed into fresh clothes, and then went walking in the jungly garden behind our small convent. In the cool green shade of bamboo and banana trees I could pray and unwind and talk over my day with God. On one otherwise uneventful afternoon there, I spied a white sphere roughly the size of a volleyball, suspended at about eye level from the branch of a large tree.

Strange, I murmured to myself. *What could that be?*

I eased my way through the undergrowth for a better look. Upon closer inspection, the object looked even more puzzling. It was partially translucent, seemingly made of a substance akin to papier-mâché, and suspended from the underside of a huge leaf. Only when I stepped close enough to touch it did I realize with a start that it was a nest of very large red ants, thousands and thousands of whom were marching steadily up the trunk of the tree, across the branch, and down into this odd globe. Their silhouettes inside the sphere, moving silently, seemed like an Indonesian shadow play with millions of extras. It made my flesh crawl, but still I watched it for a long while.

Supposing that I might have made a grand biological discovery, I announced my find to the other Sisters at dinner that night. There was a respectful pause after which the eldest, Mary Eduoard, pronounced in the Thai language four simple words that affixed themselves horribly to my brain:

"Yes. Next month. Delicious."

Seeing my uncomprehending stare, she repeated again for emphasis: "*Sehb, sehb, lai, lai.*" Delicious, delicious, very, very.

The worst part was the waiting. For several weeks, I checked the tree-cum-sphere daily, to make certain it was still in the garden and not in our kitchen. My nervousness increased with the passage of time, not knowing quite what lay in store, but convinced it was not going to be good.

Sure enough, approximately one month later, I returned home from the refugee camp one afternoon to find several local workmen with heavy bamboo poles in their hands approaching the hanging volleyball. From a safe distance I observed as they carefully dislodged the nest from underneath its leafy canopy and, wielding the poles like monster chopsticks, transported it all the way to the outdoor cooking area beside the convent. There they dropped it unceremoniously into a vat of boiling water, much to the evident satisfaction of the village woman who served as our cook. The globe dissolved with a hiss in the steaming vat, spilling out zillions of ant larvae and many more zillions of fully-grown, disturbingly large ants.

"Ants' egg soup," the cook announced to no one in particular as she added spices to the roiling pot.

Indeed, the ant larvae did look like soft little eggs, or more precisely, like squishy little gray lima beans. They looked formless enough to be edible, assuming one could muster sufficient willpower. The identity of the adult ants was another matter. Large, segmented and now lobster-red, their long ant-legs dangling in the boiling water, these were undeniably objects from the insect world and did not belong in any food group destined for a dinner plate in my world.

"But," I protested weakly to the cook, "how will you separate out the fully-grown ants from the ants' eggs?"

My question elicited only a blank stare. And no wonder, for within the hour I discovered that no attempt whatsoever would be made to separate the ants from their "eggs." We were served, not ants' egg soup, but ants-and-ants'-egg soup. This was difficult for me, and—though I tried to swallow each spoonful swiftly, to minimize contact with my taste buds—I admit to not finishing my portion. The broth and the larvae were manageable, but I left a sizeable mound of sizzled ants in the bottom of my bowl, sorry to waste the protein in all those heads and thoraxes and abdomens, but not quite sorry enough to eat them.

Nor was that the end of the episode. For one full week, all meals were graced with variations on the theme: ants' egg fillings in chicken-egg omelettes, ants' egg toppings on rice, ants' egg sauce on greens. You get the idea. Then suddenly this once-a-year delicacy was gone. Finished. It left me strangely giddy and weak, relieved that I had more or less successfully bridged another great cultural divide.

Other surprises awaited me. One evening while we were eating dinner, I heard the roar of distant helicopters. This was unusual, and I wondered a bit anxiously what sort of military maneuvers were underway at dusk, and why. Judging from the sound, there were several helicopters, and they were fast approaching our village. I wondered if they were headed for a border skirmish with their enemy—the Lao military—less than half a mile from us across the river. As I considered this possibility, the whirring reached an annoyingly loud, high pitch. Too late I realized that the sound couldn't possibly be from helicopters—the source of the noise was too diffuse now and it lacked the thump-thump regularity of rotors. My confusion mounted. What else, I wondered, could cause such a deafening whine? Then I saw it: a tornado-sized black cloud about to engulf our convent.

Locusts!

Instantly I knew the terror that Pharaoh and his henchmen must have felt at the onset of that plague. In less than a minute the swarm was upon us. Our windows, which were (O thank you, God!) protected by a fine wire mesh, went completely black, every inch covered by the wriggling, whining insects. The other Sisters glanced up briefly, and one of them got up to switch on the long fluorescent tube above our dining table, since no sunlight was now able to penetrate the blocked windows. The Sisters then resumed their meal, apparently unperturbed. Was I the only one who cared that we were surrounded and—I must point out—hopelessly outnumbered? Surely they could see that death was at our door?

What would happen next? Would we be trapped here all night? Would the locusts devour the house, and then our clothing, and perhaps us? I admit to having an active imagination, but under these grim circumstances, surely my questions did not qualify as exaggerations. Yet the other nuns were still conversing normally, as though nothing out of the ordinary were occurring. I was trying my best to look nonchalant, but was in fact rigid with adrenalin, vacillating between a feeble desire to do something heroic and the awful fear of being eaten alive.

Then the unthinkable happened. The locusts in their frantic squirming began squeezing *through* the wire mesh covering the windows and whirring into our room, attracted by the fluorescent bulb. They flapped straight toward the light, singed themselves fatally, and flopped directly down onto our dining table. Crazed little kamikaze pilots, dive-bombing by the hundreds onto our dinner plates! I used my left hand to cover my rice and my right to flick away their little corpses, having lost all interest in eating.

Now that I could examine them, up close and personal, I decided that they were probably flying termites, not locusts, since they had shimmery white wings. Strange, how clinically detached my brain had become from my body, like that of a person having a near-death experience. I sat there remembering how, in one terrifying cowboy movie from my childhood, the Indians had staked their victims to the ground, poured honey over their torsos, and abandoned them to the agonizing fate of slow-death-by-swarming-insects.[2] *Anything but that, Lord, please. Anything but that.*

The other nuns, for their part, kept talking and munching, insects and all. The room was filling up with termites, all buzzing toward the fluorescence above us, and I was barely able to maintain even a pale semblance of composure. Just then Sr. Raphael, the superior, motioned for the youngest sister to leave. She obediently jumped up from the table, slipped out the door—letting in a few million termites in the process, thank you very much—and disappeared into the ominous cloud outside.

Poor thing, I thought. *She was such a nice person. Whatever would become of her? Would we find her bones picked clean by morning?* (Not that I felt brave enough to go to her aid; no, my instincts were entirely for self-preservation. Fear effectively erased memory as well as altruism: my paralyzed brain cells rendered me incapable at that moment of recalling a simple fact from Biology 101 that would have been quite consoling: namely, that termites are not carnivorous.)

After fifteen minutes or so the young Sister returned, her light gray habit speckled darkly with clinging insects. I learned that her mission had been to turn on the few fluorescent bulbs that existed around the parish compound and to place beneath each one a large tub filled with water in order to catch the falling insects. The obvious question—*Why would anyone want to collect dead termites?*—I did not ask, for I was already feeling faint and did not want to hear the answer.

The next morning all the children were carrying handfuls of crisp, wok-roasted termites, popping them like leggy peanuts into their eager mouths. Many times that day they offered to share them with me. Many times I declined, feigning concern for them: "You need the nourishment more than I."

A few weeks later I got lucky. The Sisters had been hearing scruffling noises under the convent roof at night. Presuming that mice or rats had nested there, they called in a man from the village to clean the rafters. The noise-makers turned out to be bats. Our cook insisted on boiling and sampling one of them. Fortunately for the rest of us (well, at any rate, for me), the taste was not to her liking. And so I was spared.

Recently I was in Cambodia and was invited to lunch at an outdoor Khmer restaurant in a rural area. One of the dishes was a heap of stir-fried ants, similar to what I'd eaten when working in the Lao refugee camp. Then I recalled something I'd read about Khmer customs and so I asked my host, "Is it true that Cambodians eat tarantulas?"

"Oh, yes," he said.

Out of curiosity, I inquired, "How do they taste?"

"Very sweet, very sweet," he said. "Shall I order you some?"

I declined, telling him that I preferred not to eat spiders. He countered with the assertion, "Well, it's *not a spider*—it's a small animal!"

I disagreed in what I hoped was a polite tone: "I beg to differ. How many legs does a tarantula have?"

He thought for a bit, and said, "I do not know. I have never counted them." "Well, if it's more than four," I said, "it cannot be an animal."

That ended the conversation. Still, my brain will carry, now and forevermore, the discomforting image of a spider large enough to qualify as a small animal.

Of course, cultural differences about food exist on all sides. When refugees come to the United States, they find many of our culinary customs to be equally bizarre and sometimes shocking.

After I had been back in the States for a year or so, some of the Lao refugees whom I had known in the camps in Thailand began arriving for resettlement to Canada, France, Australia, and the United States. One of them, a young man who had been my student at Nong Khai camp, was sponsored to a town in northern California. Shortly after arrival, he sent me a short, panicky letter:

Dear Sister, please help me. My sponsor is trying to kill *me.*

Alarmed, I called the phone number he had enclosed. Once we had exchanged pleasantries for five minutes or so, a politeness required by their culture, I asked for details on the attempted murder. He dropped his voice to an urgent whisper,

"Yes, you must get me out of here. The people act friendly but I know they are trying to kill me."

I pressed him for specifics.

"They keep most of the food in a big, white, cold box for several days before they feed it to me. Not only that: Some of it comes out of cans! I am getting weaker every day."

For him, food came only in two categories: either something very fresh—still wriggling from the river or picked that morning from a garden—or else something salted and dried. In all his years, he had never seen refrigeration, nor could he by any stretch of imagination conceive of eating packaged, canned, or frozen items. It took all my persuasive skills to convince him that he was not being deliberately poisoned by the "stale, dead food" his sponsor was offering him. Only the strength of our friendship helped him overcome this huge mental hurdle.

Refugees arriving to the United States from camps in Africa face a learning curve that is even more daunting. Walking into an American grocery store is for them a stupefying experience of sensory overload—not just because there are so many *new* foods, but simply because there is *so much* food in one place. Piles of fruits and vegetables, stacks of bread, aisles and aisles of everything imaginable. Accustomed as these refugees have been to surviving on only one meal a day of boiled maize provided by the United Nations—the same monotonous thing every day of the year, year after year—the sight of these mounds of plenty literally immobilizes them. It also raises troubling questions in their minds: Why is there too much food here, and not nearly enough there? How can we enjoy full meals, when our friends in the refugee camps still suffer empty stomachs? Why is all the bounty tilted toward America? Does God favor one country over another?

Hard questions that defy glib answers. Survivors' guilt plagues most refugee newcomers. They find it difficult to relax amid such abundance when their loved ones still lack sufficient food and shelter. Most of the refugees in the United States send a good portion of their employment earnings back to friends and relatives each month.

But whether they have plenty of food or little, refugees from other cultures understand the deeper significance of a shared meal. In

2001, our Catholic Charities office assisted fifty-five young adults from southern Sudan with their resettlement in San Jose. They had lived for twelve years in remote refugee camps in East Africa, and all were dreadfully thin and malnourished upon arrival. I strongly encouraged them to eat several hearty meals each day (a new experience for them). One day I was driving one of them, Anyuon by name, to a job interview in the late afternoon. I was prepping him on how to shake hands with the interviewer, reminding him to smile and to look the interviewer in the eye and to say positive things about himself—all of which would be strange behavior in his culture.

Then I asked, "Anyuon, what have you eaten today?"

"Nothing yet," came his matter-of-fact response. Exasperated, I repeated my hope that he would at least eat a good breakfast each day.

"Well, I wanted to," he said, "but my roommates were not fast enough."

"Huh?" I asked.

"My roommates," he repeated. "They overslept and I had to go to class."

"What does that have to do with anything? Why didn't *you* eat breakfast?"

Turning sideways in his passenger seat and staring at me as if I'd just suggested something mildly obscene, Anyuon replied very firmly, "*Well, Sister, I could never eat alone!*"

His words cut me to the core. I realized how very far our American culture, with its fast-food mentality and extreme individualism, has drifted away from the fundamental human experience of meal time as social time, a time of blessing and sharing that feeds the spirit as well as the body, strengthening family ties and forging bonds of friendship.

I recalled the story told by T. E. Lawrence (better known as Lawrence of Arabia) of an incident when he was accosted in the desert by a bandit. The two wrestled briefly, but Lawrence was no match for the other man, who soon pinned him to the ground. Just as the bandit was about to slit his throat, Lawrence caught sight of the man's face, recognized him, and shouted, "Wait! I have eaten a meal with you!" Hearing this, the bandit dropped his knife, released Lawrence, and muttered an apology: "Forgive me, I didn't realize . . ." In the unwritten code of the desert, the bonds of hospitality are so strong that a person who has shared your table can no longer be your enemy.

Jesus, of course, taught this and more. He shared his last meal, a thanksgiving meal, with the person who would betray him. He often described heaven as an open banquet, a wedding feast, a welcome-home party. He specifically asked that we share meals to keep his memory alive: "Do this in memory of me." One definition of heaven is that it is a banquet open to anyone who is willing to sit down and share with everyone else. This may give us a clue to understanding Jesus' cryptic remark about it being harder for the rich to enter heaven than for a camel to squeeze through the eye of a needle. The rich, whose wealth buys them privacy as well as plenty, aren't accustomed to sharing.

When refugees first arrive to San Jose, they live in one of several transition houses operated by Catholic Charities. They reside with other refugees from a variety of countries for a few months while they learn English and prepare for employment. Among my favorite photos is a snapshot taken during Thanksgiving week in one of these houses. It shows a Serb and a Bosnian, a Cuban, a Vietnamese, several Iraqis, and an Iranian, all sitting at one table with their arms around one another, smiling into the camera. Serbia and Bosnia, of course, had fought a vicious war in the 1990s, as had Iraq and Iran a decade earlier. Around this one table, at least, those histories were being healed. The refugees were not eating alone.

$\mathcal{C}$OME AND $\mathcal{S}$EE

When Jesus first emerged from the anonymity of his three decades in Nazareth to begin public ministry, John the Baptist pointed him out from a distance: "Look, there goes the Lamb of God!" Two of John's own disciples then approached Jesus and—perhaps feeling a bit awkward and not knowing how else to start the conversation—inquired, "Rabbi, where are you staying?" In response Jesus issued the invitation that changed their lives: "Come and see" (Jn 1:38,46).

That incident from the first chapter of John's Gospel was the furthest thing from my mind when I traveled to southern California in late 1991 to participate in a conference on worldwide refugee issues. My mind was entirely preoccupied by the demands of my ministry as director of refugee and immigration programs for Catholic Charities in San Jose.

My years at Catholic Charities had been a whirlwind of reports to write and deadlines to meet, of picking up refugees at the airport as they arrived from overseas camps, and collaborating with local churches who were partnering with us to welcome them, of managing a wonderfully diverse work team of more than forty staff speaking two dozen languages, of recruiting community volunteers, and most of all, of juggling the seemingly constant crises that cropped up in the lives of the refugees whom we were resettling: medical problems (bicycle accidents, emergency appendectomies, new arrivals who collapsed and died after finally bringing their family to safety in America); family problems (difficult reunions between spouses whose lives had grown in different directions while separated by war, post-traumatic stress impeding a bread-winner's ability to hold a job, parents aghast as their sons morphed into teens with baggy pants or their daughters expected to date without an escort); cultural problems (what to do with former enemies sitting side-by-side in English-as-a-second-language class, how to help ease the pain of parents who desperately wanted to save face when their children's facility with English eclipsed their authority to negotiate the family's way in America); tragic problems (grieving parents whose decision to bring a charcoal BBQ grill into their new apartment for winter warmth asphyxiated their children); and the impossible-to-categorize problems (the foreign-born coworker who picketed my office because he refused to be supervised by a woman, the "unaccompanied minor" who turned out to be twenty-eight, the 101-year-old who wanted to get a driver's license).

I was busy with these management challenges, as well as with advocacy and direct service for refugees originating in Mozambique, Iraq, and Iran, with the ugly war in Somalia, and with the young Amerasian refugees now arriving to my office every week from Vietnam. Often I worked seven days a week, forgot meals, and barely found time to go to the bathroom. The 1980s buzzed by, and my life careened crazily along, always in the hope of doing good, but—I can see this in retrospect—seriously lacking in balance and personal attentiveness to the individual refugees themselves.

Now I sat, along with five hundred others attending this annual refugee service providers' conference, in the stately ballroom of the Bonaventure Hotel in downtown Los Angeles for the opening plenary session, which featured three panelists from overseas. Each speaker was allotted twenty minutes, but as sometimes occurs at such conferences, the first two guests went considerably over their time limit and the final speaker, an African bishop with dignified countenance and graying beard, finally got the microphone when scarcely ten minutes remained. Quietly he began telling the audience that his homeland, Sudan—a country with a land mass as large as Western Europe—was suffering from the world's longest-running civil war, that this war had killed over one million persons, mostly civilians, and displaced additional millions. He stated that his own house had been bombed more than once.

"My people are starving," he said, "tens of thousands of them. Refugee children who have escaped from prison are living in my home and in my backyard. Why isn't the world paying attention?" he wanted to know.

His words disturbed me. It had been nearly eleven years since I had begun my "new way of loving." I'd been doing refugee resettlement work for a number of years at that point. And yet I admit I knew nothing about this war or its victims. At that time the Western media hardly ever mentioned Sudan. I certainly had never met a Sudanese refugee.

This African bishop was just launching into an explanation of the situation in southern Sudan when the panel moderator stood up and announced, "Sorry, our time is up. Please move on to your next session." The bishop, silenced, stepped away from the podium, looking perplexed. Amid the shuffling of chairs, hundreds of people left the room. I stayed, embarrassed that this man, after traveling halfway around the world, had been so abruptly cut off while telling his story. I was even more unsettled by the devastation he had begun to describe.

I caught up with him in the hallway outside the hotel ballroom. "Excuse me, Bishop"—at the time I didn't remember his name— "I wish I knew more about the suffering of your people."

He gazed at me without blinking and said, "Come and see."

With those three words, the entire first chapter of John's Gospel flashed through my mind. This might as well have been a direct invitation from Jesus, so I replied without hesitation, "I will."

My next thought as I stood there (*How in the %$#@ am I going to get to Africa?*) was not so spiritual. Aside from my one year in Asia with the Lao refugees, I had never been overseas. I had no money to finance a trip to Africa. I knew where Sudan was located only because geography had been my favorite subject in elementary school, but I had no clue how I could possibly get there or, once there, negotiate travel inside a country convulsed by war. Despite these thoughts racing through my head, my heart felt completely peaceful, confident that I would indeed go.

Someone tapped my shoulder. I turned around to find a stranger. He had apparently overheard our three-sentence conversation.

Sizing me up, he asked, "Do you really want to go to southern Sudan? It's a war zone, you know."

"Yes, I really do."

He then offered me his business card. "Call me on Monday. I'll buy your ticket and make all the arrangements."

The card identified the man as an executive from Catholic Relief Services (CRS), an aid and development organization active in many of the world's trouble spots. I later learned he had been trying to educate more Americans about various unfolding disasters in the Horn of Africa, including the war in Sudan, and to that end had sponsored Bishop Paride Taban's trip to the conference.

So it came to pass that in February 1992 I found myself en route to Kenya. I had done some research by then, enough to understand the basics of the conflict I was about to see first-hand. Sudan is the largest country in Africa, its boundaries having been established by colonial-era Britain. The northern half is Arab, light-skinned, and Muslim. The north is largely a desert, sorely lacking in natural resources except along the Nile. Sudan's capital, Khartoum, lies in the north and controls the military. By contrast, the peoples of the southern half of the country are black-skinned Africans; most are animist, Anglican, or Catholic. Their lives revolve around cattle herding. The south contains the world's largest swamp, the Sudd. Much of the land there is fertile, and beneath the surface lie huge, relatively newly-discovered oil reserves.

For hundreds of years, there has been tension between Sudan's north and south, fueled by northerners who raid the south for slaves and cattle. Over the past few generations, those confrontations have flared into all-out war, pitting a heavily armed northern army with its aging fleet of Antonov bombers against loosely organized but tenacious rebel movements fighting against the army (when they aren't fighting against one another) for control of their own land. Outsiders have over-simplified the war as Muslim versus Christian, especially after the north vowed to impose Muslim *sharia* law throughout the south. Much more is involved, of course, including egos willing to obliterate their fellow countrymen and women and children in exchange for the wealth that oil brings. The senior George Bush, while serving as US Ambassador to the United Nations, flew to Khartoum after the 1973 oil crisis to inform the Sudanese government that high-tech satellite imagery indicated the presence of oil in southeastern Sudan. He then arranged a deal for Chevron to conduct ground exploration, and this eventually led to the oil pipeline whose profits helped fuel the war.[1]

But as the war dragged on for decades, it became increasingly clear that it could not be won militarily by either side. The land is too vast and rugged, too impassable during the rainy season (seven months of the year). I had heard that there was little infrastructure in the south—that roads and bridges had been destroyed. I expected to see some devastation from the years of aerial bombing, the pillaging and burning of villages, and the intentional displacement of whole populations to make way for the pipeline that now sucked oil from the Bentiu region of the south and delivered it to the north. This much I had read about in advance of my trip, but still I was utterly unprepared for what my own eyes would come to see inside southern Sudan.

My flight took me from San Francisco to Boston, where I met up with a coworker, and then on to Brussels where we slept, exhausted, on the airport floor for a few hours. As we were boarding for the final leg of the journey, I asked the gate attendant if this would be a non-stop flight to Nairobi. "Oh no," she said. "You'll be touching down first in Bujumbura."

My geography classes hadn't covered Bujumbura, so I had no idea what country we'd be visiting in the dead of night. But touch down we did, some time after midnight. Visibility from the plane was limited to the small, spotlighted terminal and a few heavy-booted soldiers silhouetted against it, machine guns in hand, patrolling the tarmac where our plane idled for an hour. During that stopover I learned we were in Burundi, neighbor to Rwanda, whose simmering ethnic strife would erupt in genocidal fury within two years.

By 2:30 a.m. we had landed in Nairobi. Staff from CRS kindly met us and deposited us in a local hotel for what remained of the night, informing us that we needed to be at Wilson Airport on the outskirts of town by 6:00 a.m. for our flight to the Sudan border. After an hour or so of sleep, we were on our way again. At the terminal we stepped onto large scales to be weighed along with our backpacks (a new experience for me). A cheerful Scandinavian pilot met us beside his six-seat plane. We two were his only passengers, the other three seats being already piled high with medicines and assorted gear. Mercifully, there was something mechanically wrong with his plane and he could not manage to get the prop engines started that morning. We returned to the hotel, thanking God all the way, to sleep the rest of the morning.

At dawn the next day we met the same pilot at the same little plane, and this time he successfully revved up his two little engines and taxied us out onto the runway. Then he turned around to face us and said gravely, "Now we must pray for a safe trip." With that, he lowered his head and spoke a fervent blessing for his plane, its engines, and its occupants. I didn't know whether to feel comforted or alarmed as we lifted off, circled Nairobi, and headed north over the beautiful Rift Valley toward Lokichokkio, squarely on the border with southern Sudan.

As lovely as the Rift Valley may be, its heat and topography induce wind drafts more than sufficient to bounce a little plane. I have always been prone to both motion sickness and altitude sickness, and I blanched with each successive lurch. As the pilot opened his cockpit window and began smoking a cigar, I, seated immediately behind him, opened a plastic bag and began vomiting. I missed the rest of the scenery. When we finally landed at Loki, as it is known to the locals, I staggered to an outhouse to splash water on my face before starting the overland trek into Sudan.

At Loki we met the CRS drivers who would take us north across the border and then westward 150 miles into the southern Sudanese town of Torit, headquarters for Bishop Taban. My companion and I would travel in two separate Land Rovers. Initially, I assumed this was because CRS wanted to haul supplies to Torit; but afterwards I realized it was because the road was considered too dangerous for a solo vehicle. I was not afraid, but I was most certainly naïve.

As we readied ourselves for the journey, I noticed a large camouflaged tent, which I was told was the immigration office. I walked over to it and pulled out my camera to snap a photo. Sudden angry shouts bludgeoned the air as half a dozen Kenyan men in full military uniforms scrambled out from the tent, one of them grabbing my camera, another grabbing me and yelling in my face. *Didn't I know it was forbidden to take pictures of military installations, especially at border outposts?* Well, no, I didn't, and I hadn't even known that the tent qualified as a military installation. He was not amused. After much negotiating—and the brave intervention of our drivers—the soldiers reluctantly released the camera to me. And we weren't even in the war zone yet.

Half an hour later we were inside southern Sudan, traveling not with official visas from the Sudanese government, but with paper permits from the main rebel group in the south, the Sudan People's Liberation Army (SPLA). The road—believe me, I use the term generously—was passable only because this was the dry season. However, that fact increased the likelihood of raids and military skirmishes. Our two Land Rovers created huge billows of dry, red dust as we jostled slowly along the rutted path. Every hour or so we would be stopped by SPLA sentries—barefoot young boys wearing scraggly shorts and carrying Kalashnikovs. They'd walk around our two vehicles, poking their rifles here and there, interrogating the drivers as to our cargo (mail, general supplies, and a few warm beers for the church workers in Torit) and the specifics of our destination. When they heard the words *Bishop Taban*, they'd nod and let us pass. At the first of these roadblocks, I gave the sentries the dry biscuits that I had grabbed in the Loki mess hall. They seemed inordinately pleased. We drove off while they were still puzzling over the plastic Ziploc container.

We drove four hours that afternoon without seeing a single dwelling or market or telephone pole or gas station or any other sign of habitation. No paved roads or signs, either—just endless scrub brush and thorn trees, blue mountains jutting above distant haze, and any number of overturned, burnt-out vehicles rusting on the side of the road. We saw no human beings other than the armed sentries until we reached Kapoeta, regional headquarters for the SPLA rebel movement.

In Kapoeta the local rebel leader, a very large, very burly fellow who looked much better fed than his troops invited us to his tent for tea, where he proceeded to harangue us for several hours. The conversation was decidedly one-sided: "Why isn't the United States sending more support for our forces? Tell your Congress we need weapons and ammunition! We are fighting for our own land. You see how Khartoum wants to wipe us off the map. They steal our women and kill our cattle and burn our villages. You are Americans—do something to help our cause!"

When we politely sidestepped his request, the commander's face hardened. He made a point of telling us that he hanged dissenters every Saturday afternoon, right there in Kapoeta, in the dusty village square. If he was trying to make friends for the SPLA, this was the wrong tack to take. We slept in tents that night and woke to the cadence of his barefoot recruits marching past at five in the morning, singing in strong unison their rebel songs.

Shortly after dawn we climbed back into the Land Rovers and resumed our journey toward Torit. Several times I begged the driver to stop along the road so that I could photograph the termite mounds—columns towering an impressive ten to fifteen feet in the air. But each time the driver told me we could not stop; we needed to press on. He, of course, already knew what I at that time did not know: that nearly every week at least one vehicle making this trek was attacked by bandits, stripped of its parts, its occupants relieved of their clothing and possessions and sometimes killed in the process.

In my ignorance I enjoyed the ride, even though the track was so rugged that I literally had to brace myself with one hand on the roof and another on the back of the seat to prevent being ricocheted around and slamming my head into the roof or the side door. More than once we had to negotiate dicey detours across *wadis* whose bridges had been washed away by flash floods originating in the mountains. After seven hours of rough driving, most of it at roughly ten miles per hour, we pulled into the town of Torit, the center of Torit Diocese and the home to which Bishop Taban had invited me.

I don't know what I was expecting, but it certainly wasn't this. Maybe I had imagined we would round a final bend and see an oasis, as in the movies where, after crawling painfully across an arid wasteland, the heroes suddenly come upon a thriving community clustered around springs of sweet water shaded by date palms. This was not that.

No, the drivers had parked our Land Rovers near a few sun-baked, rundown brick buildings and thatched huts. Huge bomb craters pitted the earth. Groups of painfully thin, dazed-looking Sudanese stood motionless in the day's heat, many wearing nothing but a threadbare blanket slung over one shoulder. It had taken us eleven hours of driving to go 150 miles—barely one quarter of an inch on a map of Sudan—only to find ourselves in a place nearly as desolate as what we had been passing through.

To make matters more interesting, it turned out that Bishop Taban himself was not in Torit, having been summoned urgently to Nairobi to press for reconciliation among some of the warring Sudanese tribes. We were, however, warmly welcomed by several other diocesan personnel and by J. Roger Schrock, leader of the New Sudan Council of Churches, an ecumenical partnership that was uniting the pastoral care and relief work of all the churches on behalf of displaced persons throughout southern Sudan. He told us there had been "some serious trouble" near Bor two weeks earlier (later confirmed to have been an army massacre of civilians that turned the Nile red with dead bodies and slain cattle), and that about forty thousand people had reportedly been seen moving away from the fighting, walking south toward a place called Ame, where they could find water in bore wells.

"We are about to go visit Ame. Would you like to come along?" Roger asked.

We squeezed into his van and headed out into the sun-scorched bush again. The heat was unrelenting. I drank all the water I was carrying in my backpack, though at least I had the presence of mind to share it with the others in the van. After several hours of driving we came to a flat, treeless expanse across which was amassed an immense and terrible throng of refugees.

These were strikingly tall people (Dinka, I was told), their height accentuated by the extreme starvation that had reduced them now to near-stick figures. Their bones were painfully visible. They were so emaciated that I did not know how they could stand, much less how they could have walked for two weeks. There must have been twenty thousand or more, stretching to the far horizon. Some were wearing rags or blankets; most were naked. Their silence was eerie. All I could think of was the scene described by the prophet Ezekiel nearly 2,600 years earlier:

> The hand of the Lord came upon me, and led me out . . . and
> set me in the center of the plain, which was now filled with
> bones. He made me walk among them in every direction so

that I saw how many they were on the surface of the plain. How dry they were! He asked me . . . "Can these bones come to life?" "Lord God," I answered, "You alone know that." (Ez 37:1–3)

Unbelievably, all of these starving people had arranged themselves into long, orderly lines, motionless under the punishing sun. At the front of each line was a man with a small notebook, meticulously recording every family's names and ages. I wondered, *Were they collecting this information for death certificates?* Surely these people would not survive much longer. I learned later that they were registering for food aid, just in case a relief convoy ever arrived. Meanwhile, there was absolutely nothing here for them except water. No food, no shelter, no medicine, no United Nations refugee camp, no aid organizations. Shock is much too mild a word to describe my state. I was numb. To this day, I have never felt so shaken.

One of the nearby sets of bones, a woman carrying an even more skeletal child, extricated herself from the line and slowly approached me: "My head hurts," she said through an interpreter. All I could do was stare at her wordlessly: *Your head hurts? Every part of your body must hurt. You are literally starving to death, your child is dying in your arms, and I don't have even a cup of water to share with you.* Barely able to overcome my paralysis (and my sudden guilt at being wealthy and well-fed), I learned that her name was Angela, and I requested permission to take her photo so that I could tell her story to the world. With great dignity she held her head up and faced the camera while I snapped the picture, and then she went back to her place in line.[2] Only after we left that place and returned to Torit did I recall that my backpack held a few aspirin that might have eased her final hours. That small forgetfulness on my part mirrored, I believe, the larger neglect of the world toward the unfolding tragedies in Sudan.

One of the more terrible aspects of the war in Sudan is that, because the land is so vast, most of its war-affected populations never get across its borders. A person is not technically a refugee until having escaped from his/her own country; millions of Sudanese have become displaced persons inside their own homeland. The difference is not just semantic. The United Nations supports many programs for refugees; far fewer resources are available for displaced persons, and what does exist must function within combat zones. Given the massive nature of the problems in southern Sudan, the United Nations funded Operation Lifeline Sudan, food convoys from Lokichokkio that attempted to reach the more desperate areas. But as demonstrated by the tragedy at Ame, it was often too little, too late.

Unnerved by the scene we had witnessed, we didn't talk much after regrouping in the van. From Ame we drove to a place called Palataka, just a bit south of Torit, to check out a school the SPLA claimed to be running for orphaned boys. The place itself had been a former Catholic compound built by Italian missionaries in the 1930s. Though now dilapidated and half-ruined, it was easy to see that it had once been a beautiful place. SPLA "escorts" would not permit us to walk freely through the buildings, some of whose brick walls were demolished; nor would they allow us to talk with the young "orphans," all of whom appeared to be in various stages of serious illness and who were only slightly less emaciated than the thousands we had just seen at Ame.

We saw listless children camped on the ground under makeshift lean-tos, too weak to do anything but stare. They were being cared for by other children. We saw many youths whose legs had festering open wounds from chiggers. All had patches on their heads where their hair had fallen out; the stubble that remained was brittle-looking and nearly orange in color from malnutrition. We passed an isolated area where boys were lying on filthy blankets—recovering from tuberculosis, according to our escorts. Other boys were taking turns pounding maize with heavy poles, or building small fires on the ground for cooking grasses and leaves. We walked through several dirty classrooms, empty rooms that contained absolutely nothing but ancient, cracked blackboards.

While our guides were explaining the glories of the education these boys were receiving from the SPLA, a few of us hung back unnoticed by the guards to talk briefly with the crowd of boys tagging onto our tour. In hurried whispers the boys explained that they were prisoners here, and that anyone caught trying to escape through the bush was physically beaten. All of them wanted to go back to their villages. They confirmed what was already obvious to us: this was neither school nor orphanage, but an ill-equipped staging ground for child soldiers in a war that made no sense.

We returned to Torit, hearts heavy and heads reeling, to interview teenagers living in the bishop's simple house. They told of having been expelled from secondary schools in the southern city of Juba after it was overtaken by northern Sudanese government forces, and then of having been imprisoned for the "crime" of refusing to change their Christian names to Muslim ones. Many of their friends had been killed, and they themselves had escaped and made their way through the bush all the way to Torit.

Sleep did not come easily that night. Now that I had seen all this, I was responsible to do something about it. In the practical words of James to the early Christians:

> If a brother or sister has nothing to wear and has no food for the day, and one of you says to them, "Go in peace, keep warm, and eat well," but you do not give them the necessities of the body, what good is it? So also faith of itself, if it does not have works, is dead. (Jas 2:15–17)

My time in Africa also included visits to Somali refugee camps in Kenya, Mozambican refugee camps in Malawi, and refugee hiding places scattered in the rural South African veldt. I listened to aid workers describing the ethical dilemmas they wrestled with: Should we give food aid when we know most of it will be stolen by the rebels, thus prolonging war? How do we ensure that aid reaches the women and children in patriarchal cultures where women have no voice? Should we send supply convoys to places where the aid workers' lives are at risk? I talked with traumatized child soldiers. I prayed with dying refugees. I walked through the tense squalor of Soweto during the week prior to the elections that vaulted Nelson Mandela to the presidency. But it was the misery I had seen in southern Sudan that haunted me most.

Before returning to California, I had promised Bishop Taban that I would not forget his people, and that I would do my best to raise some money for him. I plunged back into my regular work of resettling refugees in San Jose and began scouting out places to give presentations about Sudan. Not many people were interested. *Sudan? Where's that?* I spoke at some church clubs and women's groups and always asked for donations. Folks politely contributed ten or twenty dollars here, a hundred there. It amounted to nothing substantial.

After a few weeks, I was at the point of tears, thoroughly disheartened. What impact could a few hundred measly dollars have on a situation of such magnitude? Though I dutifully wrote personal thank-you notes to each of the donors, enclosing prints of my photo of Angela, I felt disgusted by my poor efforts and ready to give up. Anyway, it was time for my annual prayer retreat, a full week of solitude and silence during which I hoped to recoup my energies. As I packed to leave for the retreat center, I remember muttering to God, "You'll have to do something about this, because I'm leaving town."

I finished retreat eight days later, feeling somewhat refreshed, and returned to my office to find a tremendous pile of letters atop my desk: several hundred envelopes, all handwritten, from cities in the greater Bay Area. I didn't recognize any of the return addresses. I began slitting the envelopes, and out of each slipped a check payable either to me or to Bishop Taban. Each check carried the notation, "for Sudan relief," scribbled in the bottom left corner. Twenty dollars. Fifty. One hundred. Five hundred. A thousand. Who were these wonderful people? I didn't recognize any of the names. Finally, halfway through the mysterious mound, there was an envelope containing this brief note from a woman:

> *Hello, Sister. I heard you speak about Sudan last month. My son hosts a radio talk show in San Francisco. I told him about you and showed him the thank you letter you sent along with the picture of that dying woman. He talked about you on the radio last week and gave out your address in case anyone wants to donate. I hope you get some responses.*

Some responses, indeed! The checks on my desk totaled nearly $20,000. And I had done absolutely nothing—other than hand over the project to God.

Barely one month after my return from Africa, both Torit and Kapoeta fell to the advancing northern Sudanese army. All the church personnel and aid workers whom we'd met had to flee for their lives into either Uganda or Kenya. The suffering of the Sudanese people intensified, but now the outside world began, for the first time, to pay some attention to this faraway conflict. A few articles appeared in major newspapers and magazines. One national weekly magazine carried an unforgettable photo: a vulture waiting on the ground behind an emaciated child. The child's head is bowed awkwardly downward, too heavy for his thin neck, and his spindly arms are unable to balance his starved torso in a sitting position. The vulture looks larger than the child. The caption could simply have been "Southern Sudan," so powerfully did it express in one stark image the plight of the whole region.[3]

The war photographer who snapped that picture, Kevin Carter, stayed at the scene for several hours, weeping. The photo won him a Pulitzer Prize in 1994, but two months later he committed suicide. The note he left behind said, "I'm really, really sorry. The pain of life overrides the joy . . ." I keep the picture on my desk, a reminder not only of the horror of war, but of the dreadful, inescapable truth that we are all complicit.

THE *D*EAD DO *R*ISE

The phone call came late at night. The kind of call you never want to get, especially when you are five hundred miles away from home. I was standing in a hotel room in San Diego. At the other end of the line a co-worker from our Refugee Resettlement Team at Catholic Charities spoke—hesitantly at first, feeling her way like someone fearful of being blamed for bad news:

"There's been an accident here. One of the Sudanese was injured at his worksite, very seriously. We don't know if he will live."

Dreading the answer, I asked, "Who?"

She paused a long while. Too long. I stood there, gripping the phone while frantic thoughts piled up around me like so many landmines, knowing it would take just one more word to detonate them.

Then she said it: "Gabriel."

Gabriel was the youngest of our fifty-five Sudanese refugees, a person I suspected was not yet eighteen, despite the birthdate stamped on his immigration paperwork. He had come from Africa only three months earlier. He had wide-open eyes, the kind that reveal a person eager to learn new things. His very name evoked the messenger of God known for bringing good news. Was I hearing right? Gabriel was the one dying in a hospital in San Francisco?

This Gabriel could not be dying. Not now. Not after surviving more than a decade of civil war. Not after walking a thousand miles across Sudan as a five year old. Not after facing down lions and outlasting starvation and beating back sickness. Not after twelve dust-blown years in African refugee camps, forgotten and without family. Not after arriving in America—the place where, finally, he could eat more than one meal a day and where the schools would have plenty of books; where he would not suffer malaria or scorpion bites or tuberculosis again; where he might piece together a real future; where for the first time in his young life, as he had said to me just a few days earlier with a grin flashing across his face, "We Sudanese will be able to live like ordinary people."

But it was this Gabriel, the same Gabriel who already had one jagged scar on his leg. I had worked with refugees long enough to know that every scar has a story, so I had asked Gabriel about his when he first arrived. He had dismissed my question with a wave of his hand, "Oh, that is nothing," he said. "It is from the time when I was being chased by a LEOpard." That is just how he said it, in his careful English-as-a-fourth-language: a "lee-oh-pard." He explained that he had dived into a thorn bush in order to escape the animal's pursuit, and that the gash was from the sharp teeth of the thorn bush, not the sharp teeth of the leopard. Gabriel brushed it off as if he'd had a normal childhood, as if he'd merely skinned that leg playing baseball or riding a skateboard or falling off a bike. But of course, he had never done any of those things. His life had never been normal.

Now he lay in a deep coma in the trauma unit at San Francisco General Hospital. Silent. Inert. Unaware of these unnatural, antiseptic surroundings. The bandages swathing his head appeared too white against his too-black skin. There was no sound but the suck and hum of the machinery breathing for him; no color but the eerie green glow from the screens monitoring his not-very-vital signs. Foreign tubes protruded from his skull, his throat, his arms, his chest, his stomach. He lay there unmoving, while much of his blood lay dried and cracked on the cold concrete floor of a warehouse several miles away, the place where a heavy crate had fallen from a high shelf, toppling onto his unsuspecting head as he walked along. Another worker had shouted a warning, of course, but that shout was in Spanish and meant nothing to Gabriel. Had it been shouted in Dinka or KiSwahili or Arabic or English, Gabriel might have sidestepped the blow. As it was, the crate landed massively on his slight frame, crumpling him instantly into unconsciousness.

Gabriel belongs to the cohort of refugees known as the "Lost Boys of Sudan," so named because of their almost unbelievable saga of survival. News media around the world carried pictures of them in 1992 when they emerged, ten thousand gaunt and barely clothed pre-teens, out of the Sudanese war zone and into the relative safety of Kenya after months of trekking across unforgiving terrain. Following their resettlement to the United States nine years later, they were featured in articles, movies, and books. Theirs was a story of surviving, not of dying. And so Gabriel's fellow Sudanese now crowded around his American hospital bed. They would not let him die. They talked to him, though it was unlikely that Gabriel heard any of their words. They sang him Dinka songs—songs of their beloved cattle, songs about the war ending some day soon, songs of love, songs of struggle. And they prayed aloud for him: heartfelt, spontaneous prayers in their languages. God would hear the prayers of these Lost Boys.

"Is he going to die?" I asked the doctors.

"No," they said, "but we don't know if he will ever regain consciousness. It's doubtful whether he will ever walk or speak again. Until the brain swelling subsides, we cannot know how extensive the damage is."

Gabriel's friends kept constant vigil, and after one interminable month, he awoke from his coma. Eventually, after an extraordinary rehabilitation program at Valley Medical Center in San Jose, Gabriel walked out of the hospital on his own power. Hospital staff nicknamed him "The Legend." Though the accident left him permanently disabled—partially paralyzed, legally blind, impaired in both hearing and speech—Gabriel refuses to give up. He is now studying at a local college. This is Gabriel's memoir as he told it to me five years after the accident, when his recovery had reached the point where sustained speech was possible.

I am Gabriel Atem Arok, from the region of southern Sudan known as Upper Nile, and I am now twenty-four years old. The place where I was born is called Bor. At the time when I lived there—the first four years of my life—I did not know it had a name. It was simply the village where my family lived. And even during those years, I spent most of my time away from Bor, at cattle camps.

Our people, the Dinka, are cattle people. Our cattle are very big, with long, impressive horns. These cattle mean everything to us. We do not use banks or money in southern Sudan. Every family's wealth is counted in cattle. Our traditional songs are about cattle. Our love songs compare the beauty of our women to the elegance of our cattle. The toys we make as children are miniature cows hand-fashioned from clay and baked hard in the African sun.

Our cattle are the finest in the world. Parents name their children after them. Yom, for example, means a sable-colored cow with a white mark on its face. Thon means bull. Diing means a red-and-white colored cow. Yar is a completely white cow; Achol a black one. Before a Dinka marriage can take place, the girl's family must receive a dowry of dozens or perhaps a hundred cattle from the family of the boy.

Tending cattle is the duty of every Dinka boy. In the dry season, after the sorghum harvest, we boys from the village would go out to search for suitable grazing land, places with plenty of sweet grass and fresh water for our cattle. There we stayed for many months in what we called cattle camps—men and boys only—at least several days' walking distance from our village.

Each morning we used to go out from the cattle camp with our friends, to graze the young cows, walking far into the forest with several hundred cows altogether. My brother Achiek was responsible for about one hundred cows, and I, being younger, walked with him. We each carried a long switch from a tree to herd the cattle along and to chase away small, bothersome animals such as monkeys.We stayed with our cattle from noon until evening and then returned them to the cattle camp at dusk. I loved being with the cattle. My life then was perfect.

Before going out each morning we would brush our teeth with small wooden twigs; then we collected the cow dung to make our living area clean, and we saved the dung for the evening fire. If there was any leftover milk from the night before, we could drink that; but usually we didn't eat in the morning. In the evening we drank cow milk. It was enough; we felt full. If the baby cows did not use up the mother's milk, we got plenty.

In a certain season we could take blood directly from the big cattle without making them weak. In fact, we Dinka know that this makes the cattle healthier. Our elders did this by making a small cut with a sharp knife in the bull's neck, and collecting the blood that flowed out into a gourd.We cooked that blood over the fire and added a little buttermilk until it was thick like gruel.We came home only during the long rainy season, which I now know is from April until November. Back then, I only knew that much of my life was in the cattle camps and sometimes at home in the tukul with my mother.

When the sun was setting in the cattle camps, we tied the cattle with ropes to poles, and then we enjoyed our main meal of milk.Afterward, we were free to play.We wrestled; we sat by the fire; we told stories. My friend Deng Nyok told stories he had learned from our elders. Every story had a meaning for our life. I still laugh when I think about his story of the hyena and the fox:

> One time Hyena and Fox visited the home of the hyena's sister. Before they got there, Fox said, "Now let's give ourselves new names."
>
> Hyena said, "All right."
>
> Fox said, "My name will be called All Of You."
>
> Hyena agreed. But he was proud of his own name and wanted it to remain as Hyena. When they arrived, Hyena's sister cooked up a big pot of delicious-smelling food and brought it to them, saying, "This is for all of you."

Fox smiled a clever smile and said, "Did you hear that? You know my name . . ."

So Fox took and ate all of the food!

Another story Deng told us was about a fly and a frog:

A fly and a frog went to their friend's house. After they ate, they sat around the fire all together to tell stories. The friend told a funny story, and when everybody laughed, the fly laughed the most. The fly's head twisted off from laughing. And when the frog saw that, he laughed so hard that his stomach split in half. When the others saw what had happened, everyone started crying at the problems of the fly and the frog.

This story teaches us that happiness is soon followed by sorrows. I was to learn this in my own life soon enough. But at that time, in the cattle camp, I just laughed. My favorite stories were about the Fox and the Chameleon.

One time the Fox and the Chameleon met each other. Fox bragged to Chameleon, saying, "I am a great runner." Chameleon disagreed, saying, "I am a far better runner." Fox laughed and said, "Let us try." So Chameleon and Fox agreed to a race.

Chameleon found another chameleon and made a plan for winning. Before starting the race in the morning, the first Chameleon and the Fox came to the starting line. The other chameleon hid halfway along the route. Chameleon started trotting on his squat little legs. Fox sped along much faster. When Fox passed the place where the other chameleon was hiding, that chameleon jumped onto the tail of the racing fox. The first chameleon plodded along, so far behind that he was out of sight.

When Fox saw the finish line ahead, he began to relax and slow down, sure of his victory and congratulating himself. He strolled proudly toward the finish line, but just then the

clever chameleon jumped off Fox's tail and dashed to the
finish line. Chameleon won!

*In the cattle camps we had no radios or books—these are things I came to
know about much later; but we Dinka are fine storytellers, and these stories kept
us happy. We slept around the fire. We saw many stars in the African night, thousands and thousands more than you can see here in America. The cattle slept,
too. They were mostly quiet, but some nights the hyenas would try to kill the
cattle or even a lion. Hyenas travel in groups, and we could hear them growl-
ing when they were stalking a lion. Lions' eyes glow bright at night, almost like
a torch. Hyena moves easily and sees very well at night. I saw many hyenas in
Sudan. One night when I was very young, I was sleeping in our round tukul in
Bor. I woke up and looked out the window of the hut to see if it was safe to go
out to urinate, and I spotted what I thought was a small goat looking down at
the ground. But as soon as this animal raised his head—oh! It had tall legs
in front, short legs in back, and the ugly pointed head of a hyena. My fear was
greater than my need to pee that night!*

*This was my life until the fighting between the Sudanese government (that
is, the northern government army from Khartoum) and the Sudanese People's
Liberation Army (SPLA) (rebels from our land in the south) reached our area.
My uncle, who had heard that trouble was coming, told me to escape while he
stayed behind to guard our cattle. We all ran out from our places. On that day
I was with my friend Deng at the cattle camp. We all scattered. I never saw my
friend Deng again. And I do not know what happened to my uncle, either. Later I came to know that this year, the year the troubles began for me, was 1987.
I was about four years old.*

*We ran in the direction where the sun rises, and soon I met a lot of young
boys like me, walking. I joined their group. I knew only one other person. We
called him uncle, though he was not really my relative. Some SPLA soldiers
guided us. This was a terrible time. Many days of walking, always walking. I
don't know exactly, but I think it was about two months of walking. I carried
nothing. I wore only my tee shirt. No pants. No walking stick. We had to keep
walking in the daytime and also in the nighttime. When we couldn't walk any
more, we sat for a short while to rest, and then started up again. There were*

only a few women among all of us boys. I was too young to know how to count, but we were many in a long line. Maybe a hundred, maybe a thousand, maybe a million. I could not see the beginning of the line ahead of me or its end behind me.

At night we could see only a step or two in the dark, nothing more. Sometimes we held on to the arm or the shirt of the boy walking in front of us, especially when we walked through forest. No one liked those forests. Some boys were eaten by lions or hyenas if they isolated themselves—if they sat down on the side too long to rest. This happened to the smallest and the weakest boys. We heard many terrible animal noises in the night. This walking time was a very scary time for all of us. Even now, although I am a man, I feel fear when I see a forest.

After the forests we crossed a desert. That was the hardest part. No trees. No grass. No water. As a group, we carried some water with us, but it was not enough. Only a spoonful to dampen each boy's tongue; never enough to actually drink. I have no memory of how many days we spent in that desert. I do remember that I was sick afterward. It became very hard for me to walk at all. I had a fever. Even when the hot sun was shining on me, the inside of my body was cold all the time and shaking and my skin sweating. This sickness continued for about two weeks, and I really wanted to rest, but the leaders did not permit this. If I had stopped, the group would have kept going and I would have been alone. I pushed myself. No one was strong enough to carry me. On those sick days I remembered Deng's clever Chameleon and wished that I, too, could hop a ride on Fox.

Strangely, dying never came into my mind. But I saw other people dead. At the time this seemed normal to me. I heard from people behind me that my family had been killed, that all the cattle were taken by the enemy, that all the villages were burned. Still, I never thought about my own death. I just walked. It was the only thing to do. Everyone was walking. We were always thinking that we would turn back some day soon and go home after the problems ended. The soldiers said it would be better for us when we reached Ethiopia, but that meant nothing to me. I was too young to know that my own country had the name Sudan. How could I know what Ethiopia was?

I had no religion at that time, so I did not pray. My traditional belief was simply that death was death. If you died, you would join the death group, the people who had died before you. I didn't think whether that would be a good thing or a bad thing.

We walked barefoot, of course. By this time our feet were bleeding, even though we did our best to weave grasses into bandages to wrap around them. That was useless; the grass shredded and fell off after a few steps. The ground was too hard, baked by the terrible sun, and very cruel to our feet. The clay cracked into jagged pieces with sharp edges. Some people tried to crawl on their hands and knees, to make the pain less, but this was no good either.

Our hunger never stopped. We were not accustomed to scavenging for strange food; we did not know enough about that land to understand what was edible and what was poisonous. We ate leaves and roots and things that made problems for our stomachs. One lucky day, the SPLA guides shot a giraffe for us to eat; but even that was very little, for we were many.

On the way to Ethiopia, many boys died, but not the ones walking closest to me. The elders hid the corpses from us; they said it was not right for our eyes to see. But the stories traveled backwards along the walking line to reach our ears: "So-and-so died yesterday", "so-and-so was taken away by a lion last night." And we passed the words to the ears of the ones walking behind us. As strange as all this may seem to you, for me it had become normal life. I was a walking boy in a long line of walking boys. Nothing more.

One day the leaders told us we were near Ethiopia. One group crossed the River Gilo to Pinyudo; my group crossed the River Jebelrad into Dima. Fortunately for us, the river was low and we could walk across it knee-deep. There were no crocodiles in this part, not like the River Gilo where there were plenty.

We boys were surprised and disappointed to discover that the Ethiopian side of the river looked just like the Sudan side—empty of buildings, empty of food or other supplies. The elders, however, assured us that we were now in a safe place. They were right. Soon the United Nations High Commissioner for Refugees (UNHCR) set up a camp for us there. In Ethiopia we lived for about three years. The United Nations gave us food to eat. It was always the same thing—wheat flour, yellow corn, and cooking oil—but it was enough to keep us alive. In this camp—the place was called Dima—the SPLA soldiers organized our living. We went to school in a mud and thatch room; we were too many young boys—about thirty thousand—so we went to school in sessions. I went in the mornings. We studied the Arabic and English alphabets. Our teacher was very tough; if we were late even one minute, he hit us with a stick—hard! One time I was careless and lost my notebook. This was a major problem for my life. I knew that if I went to school, the teacher would give me a terrible beating. So instead I stayed away from school for about seven months. My plan was to wait until the next school term began, when we would have a different teacher.

In the afternoons the older boys marched on a dirt field, holding sticks as if rifles. They were preparing to be soldiers for the SPLA. We younger boys dreamed of the day we would be tall enough to join the fight. It would be honorable. Our elders taught us victory songs:

> We are fighting to get back our land;
> Even if they kill us, we will fight on.
> Yes, we will get back our land;
> We will not stop until that day.

Some of my friends did become rebels. They put on extra shirts to make themselves look bigger and they disappeared back into Sudan with the SPLA. The rest of us just waited in the camp for the day when we would be called to join the struggle. The elders taught us how to handle Kalashnikovs. We were shown how to take the rifle apart and reassemble it very quickly. A group of us practiced this skill under a large tree every week. The best student could complete the task in less than one minute; I was the third fastest in our group. We were never allowed to keep the rifles; we only practiced with them. We were also warned to remain silent—even if tortured—if the enemy should ever capture us. To stress the seriousness of this, some SPLA elders secretly dressed as Arabs and attacked us one day in Ethiopia in the forest. They yelled at us in Arabic and surrounded us with their weapons. We thought it was real! They put guns to our necks and threatened to shoot if we did not tell them where the SPLA hid their ammunition and supplies. Anyone who did talk that day received a severe beating.

By this time, it was becoming difficult for me to recall what the faces of my mother and father looked like. I did not know if I could ever find them again. The boys I met in Dima Camp gradually replaced my family in my mind.

One day an Anglican bishop came to Dima; he was Sudanese and he spoke Dinka, my language. I was curious, so I joined the group in their church. It was interesting.We studied the Bible. I liked it, except for the part about loving your enemy as you love yourself. This sounded completely wrong to me. Love the enemy that killed my family? I secretly believed this was impossible and that a good God would not expect this from us, but I did not dare to tell anyone what I was thinking. I liked going to church in the camp. The praying was strong and the singing made our hearts less heavy.

One day I got baptized in that church. I chose the name Gabriel because I liked the sound of it. Later, after I learned English, I read stories about the Angel Gabriel, who was always a faithful messenger of God, a bringer of good news. My heart felt very happy on the day of my baptism, and I went with my friend to play by the river all day. Since that day, I prefer being called Gabriel rather than Atem.

Our life in Dima refugee camp ended very abruptly.When the leader of Ethiopia, Mengistu Haile Mariam, was overthrown in 1991, we all had to run again.We did not understand why, but the army that took control of Ethiopia that day did not want refugees living on their land. Their tanks and their soldiers arrived suddenly at our camp, firing guns and rockets. Everything was chaos.We had no time to plan our escape.We just ran. This time the only direction to run was back into Sudan, back into the same war from which we had fled a few years earlier.

This fleeing was the scariest part of all our journeys. The Jebelrad River was not high at first, and so my group crossed easily by wading. But then it must have rained in the mountains beyond Dima, because a flash flood came and the river rose quickly. It was a thundering wall of water. Do you know what a flash flood sounds like? You cannot imagine how water, just water, can make such a sound. People say it is like the roar of a train, but I do not think a train can make noises so fierce. The sound is more like the sound I have heard in American airports of many jet engines howling at once. People who tried to get across the Jebelrad River at that time, just an hour or so after we crossed, died in the angry brown water. We kept on moving into Sudan; we did not go back. Later the sad stories came to us about the thousands who drowned, and worse, about all the ones eaten by crocodiles—how the brown river colored itself red with their blood. But everyone had to cross that day or be killed by the Ethiopian guns chasing us.

We slept on the riverbank on the Sudan side, exhausted. Then the rains came. Hard rains. We had nothing to protect us from that rain. The ground flooded up to us while we were sleeping. The water came up to our backs, so we could not turn our bodies or move our position; if we did, the water would swarm everywhere. It rained from midnight to mid-morning. By that time we were cold, very cold from the wetness. We took off our clothes and hung them on trees to dry. We waited, naked. But our blankets were too soaked from the rain; they could not dry in time. My blanket was so heavy with water that I could barely lift it. But I had to carry it anyway. I think I was about seven or eight years old when we crossed the Jebelrad River that second time.

Now we were back inside Sudan, and we were walking again. We took almost nothing. I had only the clothes I was wearing—an old blue tee shirt and gray pants that the UNHCR had given me in Dima Camp, and my one sodden blanket, which seemed to weigh more than me, slung over my shoulder. But there was one very good thing: During this part of my life, I did not feel alone. I had with me the friends whom I came to know in Dima Camp, especially Akech, who was my first and best friend. There was also Peter Jok Mabior and Daniel Mareng Jonghok. Later, in Kakuma Refugee Camp, I also became friends with Joseph Akoon, Albino Kuach, James Mapeer Agany, Peter Agwek Madut, and Angelo Biar Deng, who was left behind in Kakuma when the rest of us came to America in 2001. I do not know where he is now.

When we finally stopped walking we were at Pakok village. We stayed there for a year, maybe; I do not know exactly since I was still too young to track the months. It was a hard time at Pakok for all of us. No regular food was provided for us, and no medicine. A few times the SPLA brought a cow, which we shared among a thousand people. Our leaders carefully rationed that slaughtered cow to last for one week. Each of us got one piece of that meat, one small mouthful, with a bit of broth. That was all for twenty-four hours. We learned to survive on tiny amounts of food, less than you would think possible.

Every day we had to search for berries or roots outside: something more to eat, something to quiet the crying pains of our stomachs. But there were so many boys searching for these things in the forest that we smaller boys did not have much chance. The longer we stayed at Pakok, the farther we had to forage each day to find anything edible. We searched in small groups. By this time, we truly felt that we were already dead people, so we didn't worry so much now about going into the dangerous forest. If we woke up in the morning, we were surprised to see we were still alive. And then we wondered if we would still be alive the next day.

After many months like this, someone sent airplanes one day and dropped food to us from the sky. This was like a miracle, and our prayers that day thanked God! The planes came for three amazing days. To me, the packages looked like gigantic leaves dropping from trees, coming from so high in the sky that they looked small. But when they landed, oh! Giant sacks of food! The sacks contained maize and beans. The soldiers organized the refugees into sectors to collect the sacks from all the falling places and divide them later. The food that fell from those planes lasted for one wonderful month. That was the happiest time for us; but then, just as suddenly as it had started, it stopped. There were no more planes, no more gifts from the sky.

We stayed on in that place for several more months, once again without proper food. At that time in Pakok there came to be a lot of sickness. Whenever I saw people dying, it made my eyes more tired. Some people died from sicknesses, but I am certain that many others died from hunger. The sickest ones were carried into a little tent, a clinic that had no medicine and no real doctor. To go into that place meant you would die that same day or maybe the next day. Many of the old people—those around thirty years old or so—died. I remember one man; I did not know his name. He was lying on the ground on a mat outside the tent. Saliva kept coming out from his mouth, frothing strangely white into bubbles. His stomach was missing; the space where it should have been was instead curved inward like an empty bowl. I know I stared at him, trying to figure it out. I could see the shape of the bones on every part of his body. And all his skin was stretched too tight around those bones. Maybe I looked the same; I do not know. We did not have mirrors at Pakok. I do remember wondering, when I looked at this man, What makes skin shrink like that when you are dying? Why doesn't it hang loose around your empty stomach? Maybe these are not proper questions to consider when facing death, but I was a child then, and those are the questions I asked myself.

Too many people were dying in Pakok. What made me survive during that time was my effort to collect food in the forest every day; my friends helped me when I was too weak to walk. Really, we took turns trying to keep living. Some of what we collected was edible; some of it was not. We did not know which was which. We tried everything. Sometimes what we ate made us sicker. On such nights we suffered from terrible diarrhea on top of our usual stomach cramping. Those nights I felt certain that I would die. But nevertheless, if we found that same poison food the next day, even though it had made us so terribly sick, we would eat it again. Why? Because it did not kill us yesterday! And it was something to put in our stomachs today. Our stomachs complained loudly for the extreme emptiness. Myself, I think I survived because I did not fear death. I thought to myself, If I die today, it is enough. It will be easier than trying to stay alive.

After many boys and elders had already died, some large Red Cross trucks finally arrived to Pakok bringing beans, oil, and maize. But again our relief was cut short, because after a few weeks the rainy season began. No vehicles could pass through the swamps then. No planes could fly again to drop us food.

One night in Pakok, the SPLA suddenly roused us and told us to move toward the border of Kenya for safety. And so we began walking again, further south across mountains and more forests. By now, you might think that we boys would be expert walkers, but in fact we were thin and wobbly and weak. During the day we did not like to look up at the sky, because vultures were always circling, watching us. And at night, lions followed us. We were a long, straggly line of thousands of skinny boys with only a few men. For the lions we were easy prey.

You do not really know the feeling of total fear in your whole body until you see the eyes of a lion staring at you from the black, black night. I remember one night in particular: One moment we were walking, as usual, along a narrow path through head-high grasses; the next moment those grasses parted with no sound other than the cold breathing of a large animal. This lion was close enough to touch if we held out our arms. But, of course, we did not hold out our arms. We froze. The lion's eyes were bright and terrible-looking, strangely yellow, like deep shining urine. Its body was almost too dark for us to see in the night—but those eyes! Those two eyes seemed lit by an inner torch, a fire ready to jump out and devour us. Those two huge eyes stared at us, just stared, and then slowly, ever so slowly, they blinked. I will never forget that moment— or maybe it was an hour; who knows? And then the lion turned his head away and slipped back into the tall grass.

We were so scared! Everyone in our group trampled onto one another for protection. We tried to form a tight circle, and each person struggled to move to the innermost part of that circle. We did not know from which direction the lion would attack. Our group had a guide, and he ordered us in a rough, loud voice to start walking again. We walked as fast as we could. The lion never attacked us that night, but the memory of his eyes terrorized us for many nights to come. Why did he leave us? We do not know. Maybe there was not enough meat on our bones to interest him. Maybe he was scared off by the gun our leader carried, or maybe God saved us, or maybe we were just lucky. On other nights, at other points along the long line of walking boys (which stretched more than a mile or two), stalking lions did attack. One swift leap and it was over: a boy would be snatched by the lion's mouth and carried off into the darkness, without even a chance to cry for help.

We came to a place called Korchuei, a flat, desolate place. It had only one house. People were already living in it, but they were barely surviving themselves and had nothing to share with us. Nothing was growing there at all. No food and, more importantly, not enough water. We slept there only one night. Then we were on the move again, toward Nyiat, a small village where the people had a few goats but none for us. We slept during the day, and then headed for Boma in the evening. Terrible rains came again in the middle of the night from the surrounding mountains. There were a few empty houses at Boma, and our leader told us that we could use them for shelter. Now we were without food again.

By this time we were very dizzy from weakness. Not really thinking anymore, just walking, always walking. We found another place, confusingly with the same name, Korchuei—or so it seemed to me. This Korchuei was close to the desert. The people there had farms but certainly not enough food to spare for ten thousand starving boys. We must have been unwelcome to look at. After one night we started marching again, toward Koragarep, across a scorching, flat land. Koragarep greeted us with welcome streams filled with fish. We speared those flopping fish with sharpened sticks; it was easy because the water was disappearing, sinking fast into the thirsty ground, as we too had nearly been swallowed up by the fierceness of that land. Our stomachs were full, and we slept.

The Red Cross came in trucks then to rescue us, and they drove us to Magoth, where we received goat meat from the Toposa tribe in exchange for our clothes. Afterward, the Red Cross split us into two groups. The sickest and youngest boys, myself included, were jammed onto the Red Cross trucks; the others continued walking. Many were now completely naked. At first we were excited to ride in the truck, but as it bounced along the rough path, throwing our bodies from side to side, many of us began vomiting. We had never been in a moving vehicle before, and besides, we were too weak to hold ourselves upright. Soon the truck bed was slimy with our sickness. Strange as it may seem to you, we began to envy those who were still walking.

Eventually we stopped at the Sudanese place called Nairus. The United Nations brought food, and we began to feel almost human again. The food was only one thing—just maize—but it was good for our stomachs. We rested there; we regained some strength. The Catholic bishop, Paride Taban, cared for us. We started building huts. Before we could finish, however, we heard the terrible news that the Khartoum army had captured the southern Sudanese towns of Kapoeta and Torit, scattering the SPLA from their strongholds. This was in April of 1992. Of course it meant we had to flee yet again, quickly, into the night.

It was a dry, difficult walk through scrubby, arid land southward into Kenya. My group made it in about thirty hours; some people took three days walking, needing to rest more often. I started walking at dusk from Nairus. I reached

Lokodok and found some water there and then continued walking again. By mid-morning, I was desperately thirsty again, but forced myself to keep walking. I made it to the border and crossed over into Kenya at Lokichokkio around 2:00 p.m. The Kenyan police at the border checkpoint were distributing one small cup of water to each refugee and directing us to where we could sit on the ground and wait. That water tasted better than anything I have ever had in my life. After resting, I got three more cupfuls.

I was much luckier than the people who came later. They found no water at Lokodok—the swamp had dried up before they got there. They had no way to quench their thirst. They sucked on the damp mud. The mud only made their throats worse. But they could not delay in that place: The crocodiles were running, as they do when swamps dry up. This is what my friends told me later, the ones who came after me and who suffered more. The endless line of boys kept straggling into Lokichokkio—for three days the walking people kept arriving—thousands of us. The world noticed us then and gave us the name, the "Lost Boys of Sudan."

We sat in groups there, according to lists that our elders had drawn up in Nairus. The UN gave us sorghum to cook and some plastic sheeting to construct lean-to shelters. We stayed in Lokichokkio for several months until the UN created Kakuma Refugee Camp and relocated us there, a bit farther south into the dry Kenyan desert.

Our life in Kakuma was miserable. At first it didn't seem too bad because we didn't have to walk anymore. As time passed, though, conditions worsened. There was never enough food or water. Food was strictly rationed: A few liters of maize had to last for fifteen days. The only way we could stretch the food for that long was to take the first day's portion and make it last for three or four days. On most days we could eat one handful; but for several days in each half-month period, we had to go without eating anything at all. Sometimes the rations included a half-cup of beans, also meant to last for fifteen days. We collected the beans among our group and cooked it with the maize. If there was enough cooking oil, we traded some for extra maize. Maize could ease the constant pain in our stomachs a little. The most we ever ate was one meal per day (none on the empty days). When we did eat, it was always in the evening, because sleep is very difficult when your stomach keeps cramping. In the day-time, you can distract yourself from hunger pains by staying active, but at night it is a blessing to have something in your stomach. We never received vegetables or meat, not once in those nine years. We never had the chance.

The UN sometimes supplied wood for our cooking; when they did not, we had to search for it out in the surrounding desert. As the camp became more and more crowded—eventually it held more than 82,000 refugees from a dozen different countries—firewood was nearly impossible to scrounge. Then we had to trade some of our precious maize to the local Turkana people in exchange for firewood. To save on fuel, we cooked our maize only once every third or fourth day. We became very skilled at rationing both the wood and the maize.

Water was always a challenge, too—never enough, never easily obtained. We refugees stood in long lines at the central water tap in the camp. Some days we could not get any water at all. The UN controlled the tap. It usually took about three hours to get our jugs filled, standing in the hot sun. Fights often erupted in the water lines. Fetching water is normally the work of women, but we had no women among us, so it became our job.

Schooling in the camp was good, but I missed many weeks because of malaria and tuberculosis and other sicknesses. Most of us had the chance to attend for eight years, finishing elementary school. When we were in class, we forgot temporarily about our hunger. Our first school room was built of mud walls with a thatch roof. After one year, the UN provided baked mud bricks for the walls. Our benches were low mounds of dried mud. There was one piece of flat wood paint-ed black in each room, on which the teacher wrote. Chalk was scarce. We each had a thin paper notebook meant to last the whole year. In our third year we got wooden benches to sit on and a real blackboard for the teacher. There were few textbooks; we shared one book among four students. I enjoyed geography the most, trying to imagine the faraway places described in the textbook, places with abundant food, with rivers and trees and waterfalls, where the schools had li-braries, and the sports teams had actual soccer balls and uniforms.

I played soccer every day as soon as our lessons were done. Soccer was our release; we felt free and happy running on the dirt field. We made our own soc-cer balls by rolling up old clothing tightly and stitching it together. If the ball got punctured by our kicking, we could repair it over and over with needle and thread. We held our own tournaments with other groups in the camp.

Sometimes there were serious troubles in Kakuma. Friction among the various Sudanese tribes in the camp mirrored the fighting inside Sudan. The local Turkana people, very poor themselves, were not pleased to have thousands of foreigners on their land, drinking their scarce water and cutting down their scrub brush for firewood. They often raided our camp at night with guns. We were basically defenseless against their killing and stealing.

One day, when eight days remained before our next ration would be distributed, the Turkana came and stole all the food from our minors' compound. That was our blackest day. For that next week, we were so weak we could not even go to school. The simple act of standing caused our eyes to black out and everything to spin around and around.

The SPLA came into Kakuma occasionally to recruit new fighters. Some of my friends went back into Sudan with them. My friend Lual Deng went. I never saw him again. I was still too young to join the rebels fighting for our homeland, but we learned their songs and supported them with our prayers.

I contracted tuberculosis in Kakuma Camp but have no clear memory of it. In 1995 I went to the camp clinic and told them about my heavy cough; they tested me and arranged for me to receive a series of injections. Some of my friends suffered scorpion bites; Santino was bitten on his toe. He went unconscious and started foaming at the mouth, which scared all of us. My friends Akech and Peter had to carry him to the camp hospital. Scorpion bites are truly painful for three days, making even grown men cry.

Later in 1995, when I was about twelve, the UN photographed all of us minors in Kakuma, one by one. We did not know why. Our lives continued as usual for another four years. In 1999 a great excitement spread through the camp: The UN announced that interviews of the Lost Boys would begin for a chance to go to America. We were photographed a second time. Eventually we were called for individual appointments. The man who prepared my case file—Kamal was his name—explained that the processing agency known to us as JVA (much later I learned that this was the representative for all the American refugee resettlement agencies) would call us for a formal interview. Another year *passed before this happened to me. Meanwhile, other groups were being pro-cessed, and each Sunday an airplane landed on the dirt strip outside the camp to carry them to America.*

My formal interview was by a man who asked me about my age. I told him, "I am eighteen." I wanted very much to be eighteen so that I could go to America with my best friends, the ones whom I had been living with all those years in the camps. If I had said that I was sixteen or seventeen, the authorities would have sent me to foster care somewhere, and maybe I would never have seen my friends again. Most of the refugees were given birthdates of January 1, but the JVA man looked at me kindly and—since I clearly looked younger than the others—assigned me a birth date of December 31, 1982. The truth is that I do not know my exact age; but for sure I am younger than the age that the interviewer wrote in that report. Then the man wanted to know my story, and I answered his ques-tions as best I could. Another half year passed before I was called for a medical check-up in October 2000. The x-ray revealed a problem from tuberculosis, so my case was delayed while I took medicine for another six months. Meanwhile, all my friends left for America. It was a lonely time for me. When I finally fin-ished the medical treatment, they arranged for me to travel in May of 2001.

Before leaving the camp, I attended the mandatory cultural orientation class for three days. The teacher warned us that winters in America would be very cool and, curiously, that the rain could turn to ice. She passed around a large piece of ice to everyone in the class. This was my first time to touch ice. She also told us about telephones and 9-1-1, and that ambulances were ex-pensive and should be used only for real emergencies. Never did I imagine that I would need one myself in less than three months. She explained that our re-settlement agency would help us to find jobs shortly after arrival. I listened se-riously. Much of what she said in that class, however, seemed mysterious to me: What were apartment leases and deodorants and supermarkets, anyway? And could it really be true that women were equal to men? Mostly I worried wheth-er there would be enough cattle and Sudanese girls in the place where I was go-ing, wherever that might be.

One month later, a friend came running across the camp to tell me that my name had finally appeared on the list of refugees ready to travel. I dashed over to the posting board and discovered that it was true. My name was listed for San Jose, California, *which we all pronounced* Sanjoes. *I had no idea where San Jose was, though I later found California on a map in the booklet my cultural orientation teacher had given me. I was very excited. I gave away my few belongings. I wore a pair of thong sandals to America, and the gray tee-shirt that said* USRP *(US Refugee Program) along with the tracksuit that the US government gave to each of us for the trip.*

We flew on a prop plane from Kakuma's dirt airstrip to Nairobi's Wilson Airport. That first flight was like a near-dying experience for me. When the plane rose up, I felt fine; but when it lowered itself, my insides flopped upside down. The feeling was not good at all. I thought my heart was expanding too rapidly and might possibly explode to kill me. Finally we landed and were taken by bus to a holding center, where we spent three days waiting. That place was not clean. It had only one bathroom, an inside latrine that didn't work well. The lines were always long and the smell was awful, but we had to use it because we were in a city and there was no outdoor pit latrine such as we were used to. In that center we were given meals twice daily. Bread and vegetables and rice. That was unbelievably good.

On the third morning a bus took us to Kenyatta International Airport for our trip to America, but our jet had a mechanical problem, so the flight was cancelled. We drove back to the center and waited all day. That night we returned to the airport and took a huge KLM plane to Amsterdam. The flight was smooth. The second flight, from Amsterdam to New York, worried me. I did not like flying over the water. I knew that I could not swim well enough to reach land if the plane fell from the sky. I felt relief when we landed in New York. We changed planes again there, and now all the refugees split up for different destinations—Michigan, Virginia, Washington, Georgia. I was the only refugee on my plane going to San Jose, flying those final six hours.

The plane landed in the dark. At first, I didn't see anyone there to greet me. I got scared, so I returned to the plane. The airline worker looked at my travel document that contained information about my resettlement agency. Within five minutes, two case workers from Catholic Charities and two of my close friends from Kakuma camp, Awan and Thon Alou, arrived to welcome me. I was very thankful when I saw them, because everyone else in that place looked white to me, and I didn't feel that I belonged there until I saw Awan and Thon.

My case worker drove me to the transition house. I received a blanket and a bed. I slept even though I felt cold. In the morning the Sudanese worker took me to Catholic Charities and showed me around. There I met all my best friends, Akech and Joseph and Albino and Angelo and Emmanuel. Our hearts were really happy that day! I was many months late in joining them because of my tuberculosis delay in the camp, but they waited for me in San Jose, and we made a plan to rent a house to live together as soon as we all found jobs.

My first job, like so many other things in my life, ended very abruptly. One minute I was walking in a warehouse. The next minute—which, I am told, was a full month later—I awoke in an unfamiliar place. I could not move. My arms were tied down, and my legs refused to budge at all, no matter how hard I tried. My tongue was not working, either; something strange and solid was in my mouth. My eyes would not open; later I learned that the doctors had sewn them shut. Thank God for my ears! While the rest of my body seemed entirely useless, my ears heard the voices of my friends and the beeping and sucking noises of machinery near my head.

None of this made any sense. It felt like being dead and alive at the same time. I wondered if I had been captured by the Khartoum army. Was I in a prison or an underground torture center? But no, my Sudanese friends were in this place, talking to me in my Dinka language, singing songs to me of our wonderful cattle with their elegant long horns. I was hearing the familiar prayers they prayed for me. My ears listened as if from very far away. Slowly I came to understand that I was not dead and was not dying. I was alive. I was in California. I had survived another great difficulty.

Half a year would pass before I began to feel like a human being again. Many long months of effort in a rehabilitation hospital, working to retrain my useless arms and limp legs and to force my paralyzed tongue into recognizable speech. Six months to prove that this traumatic brain injury would not prevent me from becoming a walking boy again.

My journey has already been long, but I am no longer lost, no longer a boy. In Kakuma refugee camp I often dreamed of becoming a great scientist. My dreams now are for simpler things: to finish school; to get a job; to find a woman who will look beyond my disabilities and marry me; to become a father who loves his children. I have just become an American citizen.

Am I not proof that the dead do rise? Remember: My name is Gabriel, and I want everyone to know that my news is good.

$\mathcal{G}$OD DOES NOT $\mathcal{K}$ILL

I once attended a Peacemaking Conference in San Francisco with a friend. Our seats were near the back of a packed auditorium thrumming with the presence of several thousand people. The excitement was palpable. And why not? The agenda featured three world-famous speakers: Tenzin Gyatso, the fourteenth Dalai Lama from Tibet, recipient of the 1989 Nobel Peace Prize for his compassionate leadership in calling for a nonviolent resolution to China's oppression of Tibet; Rigoberta Menchu Tum, a Quiche Indian woman from Guatemala who received the 1992 Nobel Peace Prize for her work in furthering the human rights of indigenous peoples; and Jose Ramos-Horta, Catholic bishop and co-winner of the 1996 Nobel Peace Prize as East Timor's voice of freedom in its long struggle for independence from Indonesia. An impressive cast. Each of them gave a major presentation. Curiously, I cannot recall anything they said that day, their words having been eclipsed in my memory by an incident that occurred in the corridor outside of the auditorium during a break in the morning's schedule.

At large conferences like this, everyone mills around during the coffee break, elbow-to-elbow, threading their ways through clumps of acquaintances, squeezing toward beverage stands or bathroom lines. Being an introvert, I generally use break times to find a quiet spot where significant personal interaction is not likely to be required. What caught my eye at this event were the vendors near the side walls of the foyer displaying materials from various organizations. There were handicrafts from developing countries, a few books authored by the guest speakers, advocacy groups seeking signatures for various petitions, and, in the far corner, one long table piled artfully with Tibetan religious objects. I sidled up for a closer look. I spun the cylindrical metal prayer wheels. I studied the ornate hand-lettered scrolls. I admired the bright prayer flags.

Behind the table stood a young Tibetan monk with shaved head and saffron robe. He appeared to be about fifteen years old, perhaps slightly older. He didn't seem fazed at all by the commotion or the press of the crowd around his table, though I am sure he was more accustomed to the quiet of his monastery. I was quite captivated by how serene he looked, and I chatted briefly with him as I fingered the items. I learned that he was a refugee, as are most Tibetans outside of their homeland. While we were standing there, a well-dressed woman more than twice his age pushed past me to get his attention.

"How much are these?" she asked brusquely, holding up one of the dozen or so prayer flags neatly arranged on the table.

"Fifteen dollars each," he replied, looking up at her. He appeared happy at the prospect of making a sale.

"OK," she nodded, "But I'll need to see all the kinds you have before I buy any, so I can get the one with the best colors."

The monk bent down without a word, disappearing momentarily beneath the table and emerging with an armload of bundled prayer flags. He painstakingly untied the strings that bound them, unfurling a large stack of the banners, each one unique and hand-stitched in bold combinations of colors. Obviously proud of his wares, he spread out the prayer flags across the table. I wondered whether he had sewn them himself.

"You may wish to buy two," he advised the woman, "because it is traditional to hang them on both sides of a door."

"Hmmph," grunted the woman without looking up as she rummaged roughly through the pile. She selected two. As the monk folded them for her he looked up expectantly and said, "That will be thirty dollars."

"*What?*"The woman was incensed. "You told me *fifteen!*"

For a split second the monk looked puzzled—just long enough for a furious indignation to boil up within me. With the specter of an "Ugly American" looming, I began to feel the urge to blast this woman for her rudeness. (Never mind that I was participating in a conference on *peacemaking!*) Before I could intervene, however, the monk's face regained its calm composure. He smiled at the woman and agreed softly, without the slightest hint of annoyance,

"Yes, of course! You may have them *both* for fifteen dollars if you wish."

"Thanks, that's a good deal," harrumphed the woman as she turned sharply on her high heels and clicked back toward the auditorium.

I stood there speechless, left with the distinct impression that this young monk would have given her *all* of the items on the table for nothing if she had asked. My anger fizzled away, displaced by astonishment at the inner freedom shown by this teenager. Though I never learned his name, I will always remember what he taught me about the correlation between non-possessiveness and non-violence. I reluctantly left him and returned to the auditorium to listen to the words of the "experts" for the balance of the day.

Being with refugees in many settings over the past twenty-five years has brought me close to more kinds of violence than I can describe. To begin with, there is the violence that *causes* a person to become a refugee. For some, it is the experience of being hunted down, jailed, interrogated, and oftentimes tortured simply because their political ideas, religious practices, ethnic or social affiliation, or racial background were deemed unacceptable by the ruling authorities in their homeland. For others, it is the awful upheavals caused by war: farms destroyed, houses razed, livelihoods lost, family members captured or raped or killed.

That is followed by the numbing violence that marks the period of *displacement*, the refugee's efforts to escape from harm's way. This entails fleeing with others or entirely alone, often without even telling any family member what has happened. I know refugees whose escapes involved crossing icy mountains on foot, stowing away in trucks or ships, taking on new identities, dodging bullets, swimming across crocodile-infested rivers, and watching helplessly as friends died of thirst, sickness, snakebite, exhaustion, or overwhelming grief along the way.

Still more violence awaits those lucky enough to make their way into a refugee camp. Though camps do provide rationed food and water and some semblance of order and organization, they are not particularly safe places. Some camps are ringed with fences and barbed wire and guarded by soldiers of the host country. Others are open enclaves. Refugees in enclosed camps frequently suffer from the violence of the military sent to protect them. Rapes are common. Refugees in open camps have no defense whatsoever against incursions from bandits, rebel militias, or neighboring groups bent on avenging the intrusion of these unwelcome outsiders into their space.

My first exposure to the violence refugees endure occurred back in Thailand. By today's standards, where camps often hold up to a quarter million refugees, Nong Khai camp was relatively small—only 14,000 people. The Mekong river itself did not pose much of a barrier to the escaping refugees unless one tried to cross it during the rainy season. At some places it was less than a third of a mile wide. In fact, alongside the town of Nong Khai, the river flowed languid and green between its banks.

In the late afternoons, just before sunset, I enjoyed sitting on the Thai riverbank to pray Vespers while I watched sun-browned boys drift downstream in dugout canoes, standing to fling out their round fishing nets and pull them slowly in, arm over arm, as picture-perfect as anything I'd ever seen in *National Geographic*. But then the chug-chug-chug of an approaching metal-gray gunboat would cut through the silent scene, moving upriver while men in camouflage slowly panned its mounted machine guns as they eyed the Lao side of the river. Their idle conversations and occasional laughter would drift up to me on the bank, along with the smell of their cigarettes.

It seemed unreal, this jarring juxtaposition of war and peace. Gunfire frequently punctuated the nights. Every morning the wounded, and sometimes the dead, would be brought into Nong Khai town: Lao refugees who had crossed the river, chancing that they could elude their own government's pursuing bullets.

Fish are a mainstay of the diet in that part of the country, but one of the Thai nuns with whom I lived that year steadfastly refused to eat any fish taken from the Mekong. When I asked her why, she shrugged and sighed, "Those fish have fed on too many dead bodies."

During my stay in Nong Khai there was at least one Thai gunship attacked and sunk in the Mekong by enemy fire from Laos, and in another incident two women were killed by gunfire while they slept in their homes on the Thai side of the river. News of this reached the Bangkok *Post*, 400 miles away. "They died," the report said, "in a hail of AK-47 bullets fired across the Mekong River by Laotian soldiers at about 3:00 a.m.," for no apparent reason.

Inside the camp, where rations of rice were adequate for survival but not sufficient for good health, the refugees would do just about anything to earn spending money that would give them the wherewithal to purchase vegetables or medicines. The more educated refugees were often hired by the various non-governmental organizations working in the camp. They received small stipends as drivers, cooks, interpreters, teachers, or manual laborers. For the uneducated, there were employment opportunities in the informal economy as well, although these jobs were far less desirable. Because some of the rural roads in that corner of Thailand had been mined by insurgents, it was common practice for trucking companies who used those roads to hire refugees to walk four abreast in front of their trucks, searching for the landmines. If the refugees didn't see the mines in time, well, too bad; other refugees could replace them tomorrow—at least the trucks didn't get damaged. For this death-dodging work the refugees earned five baht per day (about 25 cents). Though the United Nations personnel who ran the camp were appalled by this practice, they admitted that they were powerless to stop it.

I remember Bounchanh, a painfully thin refugee at Nong Khai who earned money by driving a bicycle rickshaw around the camp. He rented the bicycle from someone else, which meant he had to earn enough each day to pay back the rental fee before realizing any profit. Some days he actually lost money. The tropical heat in the dusty camp was so severe that we *fahlangs* (foreigners) could not venture outdoors without the protection of an umbrella to ward off the sun's intensity. One noon, forgetting this bit of survival gear, I stepped outside the camp classroom where I was teaching to talk for a few minutes with a visitor. Suddenly what felt like a red-hot hatchet cleaved through my head. My vision blurred, I began vomiting and then passed out.

"Heat prostration, you idiot," I said to myself after being carried back to the convent to recover. "Do not make that mistake again."

Yet the refugees worked outdoors all day in that blazing sun. Certainly they were more acclimated to the punishing heat, but still they were at risk because water was very strictly rationed in the camp, and the refugees were always undernourished and dehydrated. So my friend Bounchanh earned his spare change the hard way, laboring on that bicycle, pulling one or more riders. I would see him hunched over the handlebars in the shimmery heat of the afternoon, sweat dripping off his face, straining to pull the weight behind him as he maneuvered the camp's rutted clay paths. He'd clang his little bicycle bell and wave whenever he saw me. On good days he would earn a few baht.

One morning I met Bounchanh walking toward the barbed wire fence that formed the perimeter of the camp. In the palm of his hand he was holding a small turtle that he had just purchased from the camp's open market with his hard-earned cash. Supposing that he had finally earned enough to treat himself to some fresh turtle soup, I stopped to congratulate him.

"Bounchanh," I said, "that turtle looks like a good meal."

"Oh, no," he laughed, shaking his head. "I am planning to *let it go!*"

With that, he reached through the barbed wire as far as he could and set the turtle down outside the camp, where Bounchanh himself was not allowed to go. With a contented expression, he watched it mosey slowly away.

"This turtle never hurt anyone," he explained to me. "I want him to live and be free."

His words stunned me into silence. Instead of raging against his own misfortune, Bounchanh was using his meager resources to set another creature free. I wondered then, and have wondered many times since, *what makes one person gentle and another bitter in the face of extreme suffering?*

During 1998 I worked briefly in Kakuma Camp in northern Kenya, home to more than 82,000 refugees from Sudan, Somalia, Congo, Ethiopia, Eritrea, Rwanda, Burundi, and Liberia. The camp sprawls nearly seven miles in length between two roughly parallel dry riverbeds. Each nationality lives in its assigned sector. The majority of the residents had fled from Sudan, escaping southward from that war-ravaged land. Khamis, age fourteen, was one of my students in Kakuma. Bright and eager to practice English, he followed me everywhere in the camp for a week, always—incongruously, I thought—wearing a long-sleeved white shirt. Because of the extreme equatorial heat, everyone else wore loose-fitting tee-shirts. Khamis and his family had been selected for resettlement in the United States, and I was there to teach classes in cultural orientation prior to their departure. Being chosen for resettlement meant that Khamis's family was indeed lucky. Less than one-half of one percent of camp refugees are ever selected for overseas resettlement. Khamis's family qualified for that good fortune mainly by having suffered more than most.

Khamis's father had been a medical doctor. Six years earlier, while his family was living in the Bar-el-Ghazal region of southern Sudan, armed rebels had come to their home to conscript him. He refused, explaining that he did not condone war. The rebels, not liking his answer, summarily shot and killed both him and his eldest son. The family had to flee. Khamis has vivid memories of their long, dangerous walk through the war zone, hiding by day, walking by night, doing their best to find edible roots to eat and to avoid wild animals and armed combatants. Finally they reached Kakuma in 1993, where they scrounged materials to build a thatch-walled dwelling. For safety from marauders, as well as to barricade the hut from dangerous animals, they piled spiky thorn bushes around their hut each night.

Being an open camp near the border, Kakuma Camp is often raided by Sudanese rebel militia seeking to enlist young refugees into their cause. In 1997, the very same group of rebel recruiters who had murdered Khamis's father and brother came into the camp and, recognizing the family, torched their hut in the dead of night. Blocked by the thorn bushes, the family members struggled to get out but suffered serious burns before they could break free. Khamis wears his signature long-sleeved shirt not as a fashion statement, but to hide the scars from the extensive burns on both his arms.

Violence leaves permanent marks on many refugees. Gerard, a twenty-eight-year-old refugee from western Africa, came to America in 1999. He was a third-year biochemistry major at one of the few universities in his home country when his fortunes changed. A man of firm convictions, he had been active in student affairs, advocating for better books and teachers and opportunities for aspiring students. One day his country's president decided to quash all student activism. Gerard was immediately arrested, imprisoned, and tortured very, very severely. With the help of Amnesty International, he was eventually released and placed under local house arrest. He later escaped from the house arrest (while his captors were drunk) with the secret help of a local Presbyterian minister. He made his way to a neighboring country, where he was accorded refugee status by the United Nations High Commissioner for Refugees. One year later, the U.S. government selected him for resettlement.

At Catholic Charities of San Jose, I helped to welcome and resettle Gerard. My coworkers assisted him with temporary housing and cultural orientation and computer classes. Within a month Gerard, who speaks three languages, secured a decent job that utilizes his background in science. But he will suffer all his life from the effects of the beatings he endured in prison; he is unable to stand without pain because of a leg bone that mended poorly after having been shattered. Yet I sensed no bitterness in him.

Once I asked him, "Gerard, don't you *hate* the men who did this to you?"

He looked at me, eyes wide with surprise, and then answered softly, "No, why would I hate them? They were not their best selves when they did this to me."

Not their best selves? I couldn't believe what I was hearing. When I pressed him further, Gerard explained that his torturers were military men, and young; if they had not obeyed orders to beat him, they themselves would have faced harsh punishment. I must admit that I can harbor grudges against people, sometimes for slight and merely perceived insults. I am put to shame by Gerard's ability to genuinely empathize with and forgive his torturers.

Through no fault of their own, of course, not all refugees have the inner resilience to absorb such violence without damage to their psyches. Many suffer from what mental health professionals call post-traumatic stress disorder, a condition most Americans connect with U.S. soldiers returning from combat. Something within these refugees may either suddenly snap or slowly unravel. Balance disappears. Perspective disintegrates. These survivors are plagued by nightmares, flashbacks, emotional unpredictability, and the inability to concentrate or to enjoy simple pleasures. They have simply seen too much. Their losses obscure all else. Survivors' guilt weighs heavily on them. Why, they wonder, are they still alive when so many of their relatives and friends were killed?

Merely reaching a place of safety does not mean refugees are safe from the terrors sealed in their mind's eye. Sometimes the very fact that they are finally in a safer country releases long-suppressed terrors that flood to the surface. I know an Iraqi refugee who has been successfully resettled in America for several years with his wife and children. He owns his own small business and has many friends. Still, he confided to me that he panics every time the doorbell to his apartment rings. He has to wrestle against the urge to run and hide in a back room closet, so overpoweringly vivid is his memory of Saddam Hussein's secret police ringing his doorbell to arrest him and drag him to prison.

Saddest of all are the child soldiers, like the hundreds of Mozambican youngsters whom I met in Malawi in a border refugee camp called Chiumbungame. While I was there in 1992, a nine-year-old girl was blown to pieces when she stepped on a land mine. She had simply gone outside the camp to gather firewood. The accidental death of any child is tragic enough—though it should hardly be termed "accidental" when combatants deliberately plant bombs—but even worse is the intentional recruitment of children to do the grisly work of war.

The phenomenon of child soldiers is not new, but it has reached worldwide proportions over the past fifty years.[1] As of this writing, Human Rights Watch has documented the use of child soldiers by rebel forces, paramilitary forces, and government forces in thirty-six countries spanning the globe. Boys and girls, some as young as eight years old, are forcibly conscripted as porters, cooks, concubines, messengers, human mine detectors, suicide bombers, and spies. Under threat of execution themselves if they do not follow orders, they are compelled to kill. Modern weapons are lightweight and relatively simple, such that very young children can operate them. I have been accosted by barefoot twelve-year-olds hefting rifles as they guarded roadblocks or rebel outposts. I have seen how very old their eyes look.

In Chiumbungame camp, the non-governmental organization Save the Children sponsored a rehabilitation program for war-affected children who had escaped from the civil war in Mozambique, where the rebel group Renamo had accumulated a horrific reputation for brutality and was infamous for its brazen abuse of children. Many of the youths in the camp had been so traumatized during the war that they lost all affect. They were entirely expressionless. The rehabilitation program attempted to create a safe environment, with community support from the Mozambican adults, in which the children could gradually allow their feelings to come to the surface. When the children began to have nightmares or became unruly or quarrelsome, it was deemed a hopeful sign—evidence that their rehabilitation was beginning. Then the children could start to participate in art therapy and group activities, skits in which they acted out their capture and escape, songs where they could show emotion, storytelling where they could become the small hero who overcomes great odds. Over time—for some, but not for all—a sense of normalcy reemerged. These children could then be invited into village gatherings where their past was symbolically forgiven and they were accepted back into the community.

Statistics and psychologists' reports can take us only so far, however. It is perhaps more fitting to engage in stories of real refugee children. Here are three Mozambican youth whom I met in Chiumbangame Camp in 1992.

Alberto, age fourteen, became separated from his parents when he was only nine. Soldiers from a ruthless rebel group known by the Portuguese acronym RENAMO, who waged a civil war against the Mozambican government until 1992, attacked his village, and in the confusion everyone scattered. Alberto was captured. That's all he remembers about how it began. His captors forced him to work as a porter, lugging heavy supplies through the jungle for their troops. He

lived in fear, having seen other children killed for attempting to escape. After years of trudging wearily behind the soldiers, he could
bear it no more. He decided to escape or die trying. He was successful, hiding in the bush and then walking three days westward, out of
Mozambique and into Malawi. Once there, a tracing service helped
him to find his aunt in Chiumbungame Camp. For several months Alberto attended school every day in the camp, but he never spoke a
word. He avoided eye contact with others. He ran away three times,
back into the jungle, reappearing each time after a few days. No one
really knows why. To this day, no one knows for sure what tapes play in
his head. Save the Children enrolled Alberto in its *Consoloçao* program
for war-affected children. Every day, he engaged in their planned activities, which are all geared toward helping the children deal with the
traumas of their past. The children draw pictures of the villages they
grew up in and of the attacks that ruined those places. They make family portraits of parents and siblings they have not seen in years. They
act out dramas of escape. They tell stories of clever rabbits outwit-
ting strong lions. Alberto doesn't run away anymore, and has begun to
speak. One of his first utterances was, "I saw many dead people, many
people being killed." It is very likely that Alberto himself was forced
by RENAMO to kill others. That is one of the rebels' appalling initia-
tion rites, intended to cut the children off from any hope of returning
to normal life. One can only pray that the passage of time and the loving care of others in the camp will ease Alberto's heart.

In that same camp I also met Amina, eight years old, who fled
with her mother into the Mozambican jungle when their village was
attacked. Amina's father was dragged away by the rebels. Their village was burned to the ground. Two days later Amina and her mother returned to find only charred remains. Neighbors told them, "If
you walk down that road an hour, you will see your father's head on a
stake." Instead, they fled toward the border. Three weeks later Amina's
mother was struck by lightning, instantly killed. Amina was taken to
Chiumbungame Camp, where she was placed into the care of a distant

relative. At *Consoloçao*, she is timid and withdrawn but never absent. She usually comes early, an hour before the gate opens, and is the first one to slip quietly inside.

Kalifa, a withdrawn thirteen-year-old boy with unblinking eyes, won't leave his hut. He does not feel safe outside. He refuses to play. "No, I'm not sick," he explains in a flat monotone, "I just feel sad." He is more than entitled to such feelings. After RENAMO attacked his village, Kalifa spent nearly a full day lying motionless on a cart underneath a pile of corpses, including the dead bodies of his childhood friends, all of whose throats had been slit. Under cover of nightfall, he managed to climb out of that makeshift grave and, covered with blood, disappear into the jungle. No one knows how long he had been running before he reached Chiumbungame. He never speaks unless coaxed, and then only matter-of-factly, as if reciting someone else's distant thoughts. He sits alone most of the day, rocking softly.

Sadly, the stories of Alberto, Amina, and Kalifa are far from unique. The United Nations estimates that there are at least 300,000 children just like them involved in combat today.[2]

For persons who believe in a loving God, the horror these youngest refugees endure raises searing questions. Suffering, particularly the suffering of innocent children, tears at the heart, threatening to unravel belief and unleash despair. You immediately want to do something dramatic to reverse it. "If only I were God," you think, "I would sweep the world clean of war and suffering and disease and violence and starvation and hatred and envy and greed—all the inequities that breed them." There was a time when I prayed for God to do exactly that, and could not understand why God did not obey my wishes. After all, Scriptures laud a God of mercy and justice, the Holy One who remains, in the words of the Psalmist, "close to the brokenhearted" (Ps 34:19).

A refugee is literally "one who has taken refuge." Like the author of Psalm 25, refugees implore God:

> Look toward me,
> Have pity on me.

Relieve the troubles of my heart . . .
Let me not be put to shame
For I take refuge in You.

They can make their own the words of Psalm 31:

Be my rock of refuge,
A stronghold to give me safety . . .
You will free me . . . for You are my refuge.
I am in distress:
My eye is consumed with sorrow,
My soul also and my body.
My life is spent with grief . . .
I am forgotten like the unremembered dead.
I am like a dish that is broken . . .

The following excerpt from a letter sent to me by a refugee mirrors the anguish of those Psalms written during the Exile of old:

My sorrow is not finish.
I cannot write all of it to you.
I am like a bird in a cage.
Sometime I want to die
for escaping all of the injustice in the world.
My heart is almost broken,
thinking of my parents, my children, what future?
God makes everything;
Some day maybe He will make me
to have a good life.

Why does there seem to be no divine response to their plight? The more involved I became with refugees, the more insistently this question gnawed at me: "What does God have to say about the violence that refugees endure?" I'm not sure that this question will ever have an adequate answer. But the following paragraph, written by an anonymous political prisoner and quoted in a magazine devoted to social justice, reframes the issue somewhat:

I was in a torture center, imprisoned in a small, narrow cell without light or sanitary facilities. When they opened the door, letting in a little light, I could see many inscriptions on the walls. One day they left the door open a little longer than usual, and when I looked closely around the cell I saw, on one wall, a big blood stain. Below it, written by a finger dipped in the blood, it said, "Dios no mata"—God does not kill. This is something that is burned in my memory and will be with me the rest of my life.

—an Argentine prisoner[3]

To all our questioning about the existence of evil and violence, God gives one simple response: I do not kill. The violence that plagues the world is not God's doing. Throughout the scriptures we see this truth restated over and over: "I have set before you life and death . . . choose life" (Dt 30:19). "They call him Wonder-Counselor, Father Forever, Prince of Peace. His dominion is vast and forever peaceful" (Is 9:5–6). "My thoughts are only of peace" (Jer 29:11). "I will not give vent to my anger . . . for I am God, not man, the Holy One present among you; I will not let the flames consume you" (Hos 11:9).

Jesus says that his deepest desire, the very purpose of his life, is to be the source of abundant life for all: "I came so that they might have life and have it more abundantly" (Jn 10:10). "Come to me, all you who are weary and find life burdensome; come to me, and you shall find rest" (Mt 11:28). "Behold, I am with you always, until the end of the age" (Mt 28:20).

The words most often spoken in the Christian Scriptures are greetings of peace—for example: "While they were still speaking . . . he stood in their midst and said to them, 'Peace be with you'" (Lk 24:36). "I have told you this so that you might have peace in me. In the world you will have trouble, but take courage, I have conquered the world" (Jn 16:33). "May the God of hope fill you with all joy and peace in believing, so that you may abound in hope by the power of the holy Spirit" (Rm 15:13). "For he [Jesus] is our peace, he who made [us] one and broke down the dividing wall of enmity" (Ep 2:14). "Then the peace of God that surpasses all understanding will guard your hearts and minds" (Phil 4:7).

Faced with conflict, violence, persecution, and death, the early Christians clung tenaciously to their vision of a world where enemies would reconcile and peace would flourish.

I suspect that great suffering gave rise to the idea of "a leap of faith." When all else is lost, maybe that leap brings us, beyond all reasonable expectations, to the very heart of divine consolation. And I suspect that the holiness of the few who have taken that leap and now live in God's heart may be all that holds together a world otherwise reeling in pain. As the poet Jane Hirshfield wrote:

> So few grains of happiness
> Measured against all the dark;
> And still the scales balance.[4]

The scales do balance—and some day might even tip toward a new way of loving.

CREATURE
DISCOMFORT

Eighteen months after returning from my time in the Thai refugee camp, but still long before neighborhood gentrification reached
the more dilapidated areas of New York City, I spent some time in East
Harlem. I remember its tired tenements—how they leaned away from
one another, as if weary of company—and how the sidewalks cracked
unevenly under the moldering weight of garbage and the slow, heavy
steps of the homeless. I can still smell the fires they nursed to warm
themselves. Rodents, not yet banished underground, surely outnumbered the residents of our block; they did not skitter but only stared at
my intrusive comings and goings. Decay seeped from the empty lots
strewn with bottles emptied of cheap wine. Even the trees, defeated
by concrete that sliced off sun, slumped in their small patches of dirt,
their limbs nearly as gray and bare as the tails of the rats.

Each month a professional exterminator inspected the weathered
brick convent where I was living. He was a grizzled fellow, quiet and
of indeterminate age. During his monthly rounds he sprayed our base-
ment with pesticides. I could not imagine a job more miserable than

his: spending every day poking under other people's sinks and cabinets and rugs, looking for rat droppings, roaches, and spider infestations. Yet he seemed kindly. He dressed in loose-fitting overalls, flannel shirt, and old boots and went about his work in a deliberate, unhurried way. I struck up a conversation with him one day as he crouched to peer behind our washing machine.

I asked whatever had possessed him to choose this line of work. He smiled a contented smile, rocked back on his heels, tipped his baseball cap back slightly, and answered, "Sistah, there be some men, they like to *hunt*." He paused for emphasis, his eyes fixed on a point far away—he then added with a satisfied nod, "Sistah, I be a *hunter*!"

For some time thereafter in my mind I imagined him at home in the evenings after work, contentedly smoking an old pipe and reading the daily news beneath the trophy heads of gigantic roaches stuffed and mounted on his den wall above the fireplace, their eyes bugging out and their antennae poised to scan the room for scraps of food. It still gives me the willies.

In fact, anything involving bugs gives me the willies—above all, anything involving spiders.

I am unreasonably afraid of spiders. My fear is not merely squeamishness—it is a heart-stopping, muscle-freezing paranoia. I have tried to talk myself out of it, but the loathing remains immune to logic. I chide myself: *Most spiders cannot harm me; after all, my brain is larger, and I outweigh them.* I am even willing to concede, grudgingly, that spiders might serve a useful purpose in some awful, arachnidan way. Certainly they are part of the complex miracle of creation and, for that fact alone, deserve some respect. But none of this theoretical inner monologue has the slightest chance of dislodging the primal dread that grips me at the sight of an *actual* spider, or even the sight of a suspicious smudge on the wall that might, under brighter light, reveal itself to be an actual spider.

This neurosis has deep roots. During my childhood our family lived at the edge of a new suburb in California. Our backyard bordered on wooded hills dense with undergrowth and eucalyptus trees. The place was perfect for running and climbing and hiding, for building forts and playing cowboys-and-Indians with my brothers and all the other kids on the block. However, the proximity of the woods to our house had one major drawback: these woods in which we loved to play were also the sinister breeding ground for spiders, who crept unbidden into our otherwise secure home.

I could never reconcile myself to the sight of black spiders on our white carpet. Too phobic to remove them myself, I devised a scheme for self-protection, one that tempered my anxiety and at the same time spared our carpet the messiness of murder-by-blunt-instrument. The plan was straightforward: I saved and washed and stashed under my bed many small plastic containers that had once held cottage cheese or margarine. These I carefully upended over each unsuspecting, unforgiven trespasser. Then I hurriedly piled two or three heavy books on top of each tub, guaranteeing that even the strongest spider could not somehow muscle its way out.

By the time my brothers came home in the afternoon, there would be several of these spider dungeons scattered about the house. I would beg my brothers to dispose of the prisoners. Sometimes they willingly did the deed; otherwise, I pledged future favors. I confess that I went so far as to promise to bake them cookies or clean their room—anything to coax compliance. My need for their continuing cooperation forced me to stay on good terms with them. Who knows? Perhaps it kept our family together.

In other areas of life I have little fear. I've handled snakes without flinching, gone willingly into active war zones, and once captured a burglar who broke into our convent. I am generally calm in dangerous situations. Unless, of course, the situation involves a spider. In such circumstances (when I am without plastic tubs or helpful brothers) my only recourse is combat. All my noble desires to live non-violently, all my promises to treat creation with reverence, all my ability to think rationally—gone! It is spider versus me. Only one of us will live. You would be correct in deducing that I have committed deadly deeds. Many times.

This, then, is my personal proof of the existence of God, equaling any of Aquinas' sophisticated thoughts on the subject: When involved in refugee work, especially in places where spiders grow to unnatural sizes and can inflict real harm on the unwary, my fear of them diminishes to the point where I can continue to function. This was not a change likely to occur without divine intervention.

Consider my very first day in Nong Khai refugee camp. One of the refugees, Syda by name, offered to tutor me in the Lao language. The two of us were sitting together on a rough bamboo bench in a small hut used by teachers in one of the camp's elementary schools. A large, tattered map of Southeast Asia hung nearby, tacked onto the mud wall near my elbow, its edges curled forward in the intense heat of the day. As I bent over the wondrous Sanskrit-based curlicue script that Syda was patiently teaching me, I spotted movement from the corner of my eye. Something dark and massive and hairy emerged from the thatched roof and crept down onto the map, covering almost the whole of Thailand. I froze. My tutor continued on with the lesson, though he was obviously aware of this monstrous thing—by far the most enormous spider I'd ever seen. I glanced nervously down at my now-paralyzed hand clutching in a death grip its wooden pencil, and then looked directly up at the spider, verifying to my dismay that its body was indeed larger than my fist.

Syda, like most of the refugees in that camp, was a practicing Buddhist who avoided harming living creatures. He looked up at the beast, which by now was hulking deliberately toward China, and announced to me in a bright, helpful tone,

"If you eat this spider, it will cure bed-wetting."

Thankfully, bed-wetting was not a problem I suffered from; but I felt instant empathy for all children growing up in northeast Thailand.

Meanwhile, Syda's sentence cycled impossibly, over and over again, in my poor head: "If you eat this spider . . . If you eat this spider . . ." One part of my brain absolutely refused to comprehend any sentence in which the verb "eat" was connected to the object "spider." Yet that was exactly what Syda had said, wasn't it? The other, more stupidly stubborn part of my brain refused to let go of the specter suggested by his words. Sweat trickled off my forehead— I could not tell whether from raw fear or from the humid air now claustrophobically crowded by the slow extension of those eight hairy legs. Silently I asked God if I had made a grave mistake in coming here.

My tutor had already turned his attention back to the lesson plan, seemingly indifferent to this clear and present danger. I sat there immobilized, at once hyper-alert and yet so shuttered by fear that I heard nothing further that Syda was saying. It was precisely then that the miracle occurred. Boosted by an unexplained infusion of courage, I shifted on the bench so that the monster was out of my line of sight, behind my shoulder. It required an act of immense willpower, but I deliberately returned to my study of the Lao alphabet. To this day, I consider it one of my bravest moments. Let that spider conquer continents or scare young boys into continence! It would not prevent me from wrestling with the thirty-eight vowels and forty-eight consonants in the first-grade textbook whose rumpled pages lay open before me.

During the year I worked in Nong Khai, I gradually learned to coexist (really, what choice did I have?) with a large percentage of the entomological world. By the transforming grace of God, I realized over time that this northeastern slice of Thailand was *their* place, not mine. I was the intruder, not vice versa.

One morning I was listening from my upstairs bedroom to the early chants rising from the Buddhist monastery across the road from the convent where I lived. I stood at the window idly watching young Thai children, impeccably dressed in their crisp blue shorts and white blouses, as they walked to school. I noticed one girl, perhaps five years old, walking very slowly along the dirt path with one arm stretched behind her. When she came closer I could see that there was a thin leash attached to her hand, much like what would be used to walk a small dog, but at first I couldn't see any pet. Then I noticed sunshine glinting off some hard, shiny surface inching along several feet behind her. I finally spied the source—a huge scarab beetle tied to the end of the string. She was walking a beetle to class! Even from a distance, it looked disturbingly large. *Aauugh*, I groaned to myself. *What kind of a place* is *this?* My unbelieving Western eyes winced when the child casually turned backwards, picked up the gleamingly-green iridescent creature and placed it tenderly on her shoulder. Didn't anyone here realize that bugs and people should at least maintain safe distances, if not separate universes?

Since I did not speak Thai and the nuns with whom I lived did not speak much English, it was often a challenge to determine exactly what the plan was for any given day, especially when we piled into the convent van for an outing. I'd politely inquire, "Where are we going?" and their reply was usually a vigorous nodding of heads, "Yes! Yes!"

One night we drove about half an hour to the neighboring village of Vieng Khuk, where the local Catholic parish was celebrating a jubilee. The small church was crowded with villagers by the time we arrived, but they made room for us to squeeze in. Kneeling in the dimly lit church, my senses lulled by the lovely Thai singing and the comfortingly familiar smells of incense and bees' wax candles, some time passed before I noticed the curiously blotchy design on the cracked linoleum floor. (I'm the sort of person who compulsively analyzes geometric patterns on the floor tiles at other people's houses and calculates the number of holes in acoustic ceiling panels whenever I am at the dentist.) The floor pattern in this particular church seemed creatively irregular, so I put on my glasses and squinted underneath the pews in front of me, searching for the place where the randomness would begin to repeat, as printed patterns always do. Much to my dismay, the pattern instead appeared to shift, re-arranging itself as if by some unseen black-and-white kaleidoscope. Only then did I realize, with no small amount of horror, that the floor was in fact thick with bugs crawling, hopping, flitting, and scooting, a mere two inches beneath my kneeling body!

I looked anxiously around, my pulse racing ahead of my thoughts. All the others in the church appeared unaware of this creeping terror. They continued chanting in unison from their prayer books as the liturgy proceeded. I, on the other hand, my breathing coming fast and shallow, felt exactly like the murderer in Edgar Allen Poe's *The Telltale Heart*. My attention was focused entirely on the dreadful reality below me. *Did no one else see them? How could they not? But no one else is even flinching!* Kneeling—balanced on a plank so that my bare toes did not touch the ground—I learned that night how endless a Benediction service can be. My own prayer, I'm afraid, never rose above fervently repeated mantras that those thousand jumping, buzzing, whirring black things would not find their way under the cotton skirt that I was now wrapping ever more tightly around my legs.

I was the first one out of the church when the service finished, exhaling an immense sigh of relief. But once the congregation emerged, we were all given lighted tapers to carry aloft for a procession. The tiny flames attracted open-air swarms of night-flying creatures. We were treated to an almost comic onslaught of gnats, mosquitoes, floppingly large moths, and bats swooping down on us from the inky sky. It's a wonder, really, that I didn't give up religion.

On another of our memorable trips in the van, we were riding south from Nong Khai on a sunny afternoon to the town of Udon

Thani. As always, I reveled in the passing scenery, imagining how my favorite painters might have rendered the bright green rice fields, the stilted wooden houses, and the distant orange-and-gold pagodas with their trim, upturned roofs petitioning the sky.

Would van Gogh have invented a dense pigment for the black-flanked water buffalo? Would Gauguin have delighted in the unself-conscious loveliness of the women selling mangoes by the side of the road? Would Klimt have found ways to make these scenes shimmer liquidly in the noonday sun? Occasionally we passed an elephant, down from the heavy work of hauling teak logs in the forest. No matter which direction I looked, there was something new to see.

At one point, I glimpsed what appeared to be giant pieces of cheesecloth slung over the telephone wires and stretching fifteen to twenty feet in length. A few kilometers further along the road, I saw the same thing again.

"Why do they drape cheesecloth along the telephone wires?" I asked.

No answer from the nuns in the van.

By now, I had learned that when my questions went unanswered, it usually meant that there was something wrong with my question, something that didn't match their way of looking at life. I suspected it was the word "cheesecloth." I was mistaken.

"What is *that?*" I inquired again, pointing to the long graceful folds of cloth looping from pole to pole.

"Oh, spider webs," came the casual reply.

Spider webs! Spider webs three times the size of our van? No, this could not be happening. This assaulted my sense of what was right and proportional in the world. A shudder ran through me. Luckily, I never actually *saw* those spiders (thank you, God, for this small favor). Nevertheless, hugely malevolent "cheesecloth creatures" menaced my sleep for several weeks.[1]

Years later, after returning to the United States, I chanced upon a *Far Side* cartoon drawn by Gary Larson. It showed two plump toddlers on a playground, one climbing up the stairs of a slide, another poised at the top ready to glide down. A large, ropy spider web spanned the bottom of the slide. Two spiders stood to the side, eyeing the children and sneering: "If we pull this off, we'll eat like kings!"

I wondered, *had Gary Larson ridden on that same road to Udon?*

Because of the tropical heat in Thailand, I wore sandals most of the time, but quickly learned never to stand motionless without lifting my feet every few seconds. Otherwise, the ever-present swarms of ants would conclude that my legs were columns to be climbed and conquered. I am not referring only to outdoor settings. Every night, military platoons of ants—red ants, black ants, tiny ants, large ants—commandeered my second-floor bedroom, marching in bold phalanxes five to six inches wide across whatever lay in their way. Of course, I am not afraid of an ant; but there is something deeply unsettling, even downright ominous, about tens of thousands of ants, organized and on the move. Besides, I had seen their anthills out in the fields— huge swells of earth larger than human burial mounds—and wondered uneasily what lay beneath.

A sturdy little broom rested by my bed so that in the mornings I could sweep for myself a path over to the chair on which my clothing hung. Gecko lizards, whom I considered my dearest friends that year, kept the room from being overrun by more distasteful creatures. Besides providing protection, the geckos entertained me with the laughing noises they emitted all night long: Taking a deep breath and holding it in the sac-like pouch beneath their chin, they would let the air out in gradual spurts, "HA, HA, Ha, ha!" At one point during the year, all the geckos disappeared from my bedroom, allowing the insect quotient to reach alarming proportions. I was nearing panic by the time they returned, this time with lots of little gecko offspring in tow, trying out their baby-sized nocturnal chuckling. I slept well from then on.

Still, the smallest bit of carelessness could have unwholesome consequences.

My bed, to be sure, had defensive moats around it in the form of a small bowl of water under each leg, to prevent the insect world from scaling those legs and sharing my cozy, mosquito-netted cot. Likewise, in the dining area of the convent, the single wooden cabinet that contained crackers, fruit, and other food was undergirded by four bowls of water. One memorable afternoon I returned from the refugee camp, tired and sweaty, only to enter a scene lifted straight from a Hollywood horror flick: Where the food cupboard had stood that morning, there stood now only a five-foot-tall, seething, crawling, massive ant-edifice. True, the shifting dark nightmare was in the *shape* of the food cabinet, but I couldn't see the wood at all. I stood there, transfixed by the scene, not quite grasping what had happened, not wanting to let this picture imprint itself on my helpless brain, yet unable to look away.

After a moment of total stupor, the awful truth dawned: Someone had forgotten to refill the water in the bowls that morning. The jungle had taken over in the space of half a day. Needless to say, this impressed me vividly. I filled those little life-saving bowls in my bedroom religiously twice a day after that.

In later years, as my work took me to new continents and new refugees, I encountered even more hideous six- and eight-legged adversaries that further tested my resolve. On several occasions I have spent time at Kakuma Refugee Camp in Kenya, just south of the Sudan border. A more desolate, windswept place would be hard to imagine. About 82,000 persons displaced by war make their lodging in that barren landscape—a place with insufficient water, food, or facilities, blasted by searing desert heat and sandstorms fierce enough to choke living things.

As is my habit whenever I enter a new refugee camp, I inquired as to what particular danger I should try to avoid. Responses varied from camp to camp: sometimes contaminated water, sometimes poisonous snakes, or encroachments by armed rebels. I learned that Kakuma Camp was infamous for its camel spiders. Kakuma was precisely the type of place where only a desert-hardened spider would choose to live.

"How will I know which spiders are camel spiders?" I asked, picturing in my mind's eye a shaggy, double-hunchbacked bug with knobby kneecaps.

"Oh, you will know," came the reply from an experienced camp worker, "by their size and their speed. All you'll see is the blur going by." Then she added, as if to comfort me, "They don't have humps. They're named for their color."

I have since discovered that camel spiders—also known as wind scorpions because of their speed—are technically not spiders at all, but rather solifugids, a biological classification approximating a frightful cross between a spider and a scorpion. Camel spiders have been described as looking like blond tarantulas, but twice the size. They have a claw-like mouth in front and the ability to move so fast that the human eye cannot follow them. A *National Geographic* article summed up their attributes: "Quickness, aggressiveness, and body-crunching jaws make the wind scorpion a triple threat."[2]

Camel spiders grow to nearly six inches in length and can dash ten miles per hour. Humans cannot outrun them. They prefer shade to sunlight. They tend to become fiercely aggressive when cornered. These are facts I wish I had known while staying in Kakuma camp.

While teaching classes to the refugees in that dusty corner of Africa, I regularly scanned the sandy, camel-colored ground for hefty, camel-colored blurs. By night I used a tiny flashlight to see where I was stepping. Days passed without my encountering anything worse than malarial mosquitoes and a few regular scorpions (unless, of course, you count the murder of a refugee one night by the neighboring

Turkana tribe, the subsequent riot in the camp protesting the over-
all lack of security, or the near-stoning of a refugee accused of stealing
someone's bicycle). On Sunday morning, however, as I was preparing
to open the ill-fitting wood plank door of my borrowed hut to go out
into the bright sunshine to the camp church, I noticed a four-inch solid
"wedge" blocking out the light between the door and the door frame,
just above the knob. Upon closer inspection, the wedge showed itself
to have legs. Camel-colored legs. My heart plunged down to my toes. I
was face-to-face with a camel spider who just happened to be between
me and my only exit.

What to do? There was no one within hailing distance. (Where was
my steady New York exterminator-hunter friend when I needed him?)
Fighting back panic while keeping one eye on the wedge—because
I knew if it sprang into the room, I wouldn't be able to find it, and
then I wouldn't be able to live there any more—I backed up into the
room to search for a suitable weapon. First, I inched out of my sandals
and pulled on my running shoes, with a view toward that hoped-for
moment when running would be possible. Then I cautiously approached the door, my trusty semi-automatic sandal in hand. It would
be a fight to the death. On the Sabbath, no less.

The way I saw it, I had a fifty-fifty chance of survival.[3] When I
opened the door, the creature would either leap into the room (perhaps onto me, a prospect too terrible to contemplate) or else outward into its natural desert environs. Wouldn't a sensible spider go
outdoors, where it belonged? No, of course not. The instant I twisted the knob and kicked open the door, the wedge jumped toward me,
skidding onto the floor and zooming to a dark corner of the room to
crouch behind a stack of empty Coke bottles left by the room's previous tenant. I could see its heaving mass, magnified terribly (as if it
weren't scary enough already) through the thick glass of the bottles,
like some wiggly-mirror fun-house prop. But this was no joke.

Long, tense moments followed while both of us considered our
options. I began gingerly toppling the bottles one by one with the tip

of my sandal until we two sorry creatures eyed each other directly. Then, with its line of defense half-dismantled, the spider made a desperate dash across the room. And I, close to fainting from having held my breath so long, threw my lethal sandal several feet beyond that scrambling blur with all the force I could muster, timing it so that the blur and the sandal met at the same point. ("Never skate to where the puck is," said a famous hockey player. "Skate to where the puck is going to be.") All my childhood years of playing baseball had primed me for this one fateful pitch.

There is now one less solifugid in the world.

I'm not proud of how my encounters with spiders reveal a violent streak in me, but it is real. And though I try not to harm other types of creatures, I still feel incongruously imperiled by the spiders of the world and, therefore, almost justified in my first-strike attitude toward them.

Contrast this with the experience of my friend, Ahmed, a young refugee who spent four years imprisoned in the Middle East after having been arrested for his political beliefs. Ahmed told me how difficult it was not to sink into despondency while suffering in that damp, dark hole, day after day, month after month, year after year. The physical isolation, the nightly interrogations and beatings, the complete lack of sunlight, the unrelenting stench of human waste, the miserable half-cup of rancid rice each day—it was almost too much to bear.

Then one day a large spider unexpectedly appeared in his prison cell. Ahmed says that this simple evidence of life delighted him beyond all reason. He talked to the spider. He played with it. He watched its meanderings. He even swears that once, when the spider bit his arm, its venom cured an open sore that had been festering for weeks. Most of all, Ahmed drew courage from the realization that one other living creature, besides his torturers, knew where he was. He told me that he praised Allah often for the brotherhood he felt with that spider,

149

who was for him a messenger of hope from the outside world. Ahmed is now resettled, living safely in the United States. To this day, he says he still views every spider as a welcome friend.

Ahmed's story makes me embarrassingly aware of the absurdity of my own phobia. All the same, I cannot completely rid myself of the instinctive urge to preemptively kill crawly things before they kill me.

My fear, irrational as it is, makes me a bit more understanding of others who lash out at things or people. I suspect that those who harbor deep hatreds or act violently must feel somehow threatened. When faced with such feelings, it takes great inner strength to be gentle. Perhaps the world would be a more peaceful place if we'd all do what we can to help others recognize their own competence and their own goodness. Maybe that will lead to a bit more tolerance in our troubled world.

Still, one thing is sure: When I get to heaven, if God has eight legs, I am in very big trouble.

THIS *FLOWING* TOWARD *ME*

While much of my adult life has been about trying to cultivate a new way of loving, no one who knows me would ever call me sentimental. I have, in fact, a painfully sensitive inner Geiger counter for detecting schmaltz. If a book or movie or conversation contains too much unwarranted emoting, I start to squirm. Where possible, I quickly exit stage left. Perhaps this is because I was raised with four brothers in an easy, rough-and-tumble sort of way, where sarcasm qualified as endearment, and a gentle shove to the shoulder marked the upper limit in showing sibling affection.

In addition to guarding its emotions, my family also guarded its privacy. As a child, I noticed my parents' annoyance at having to answer what were, to them, intrusive questions once every ten years for the national census. "How many persons live here?" and "Are you employed outside the home?" seemed entirely too intimate to be released beyond our tight family circle, much less made available to anonymous government clerks. We were private people.

Being reserved and keeping my feelings to myself, therefore, comes naturally to me. I entered a convent expecting a quiet, ordered life. I taught high school math, where most problems had a neat solution. My daily schedule was quite predictable. Imagine my surprise, then, when into this rather staid, undemonstrative life stepped a God who dances. I remember the precise moment it happened. I had recently completed a thirty-day retreat, a once-in-a-lifetime opportunity during which I set aside the responsibilities of my normal routine and entered into a space cleared out, as it were, for God alone. If this sounds strange or burdensome or even mildly scary, don't worry; it just means that God is not inviting you to such an experience at this point in your life. But if it touches something resonant within you, if you feel an attraction tugging you in this direction, if you sense your heart saying, "Oh, I wonder if I could ever do something like that," then shelter that desire as you would a young seedling from frost and wait for the time when the yearning wends its way toward the surface of your life, where it might lead you toward a retreat center or a quiet park or a corner of your bedroom for an hour or a day or a week or even a month of listening to the One who drew you there.

All the great religious traditions extol the silence in which retreats are steeped. Noise too readily distracts us from that deeper inner place where (usually unbeknownst to us) our hearts remain always attentive to God. I imagine this place of attentiveness to be like the tiny pilot light found in every water heater, a little flame that never goes out—what Europeans charmingly call a "wake flame." When was the last time you thought about the pilot light in your house? Yet it's always there. Likewise, hidden in us there exists a single small point of adoration fixed on God. Thomas Merton called it *le point vierge*, the part of ourselves that is forever, no matter what, true to the God who tends the flame. Nothing we either do or fail to do can dislodge it or extinguish it—not busyness or resistance or neglect or wrongdoing—because it is God's work, not ours.

The prophets of old groped for ways to voice God's unshakeable persistence in loving us and jealously shepherding that spark of original communion buried beneath the general commotion within us. Writers like Isaiah, Jeremiah, Hosea, and Zephaniah employed successively bolder images in the Hebrew Scriptures to communicate this truth we find so hard to believe—that we are precious in God's sight; that God mothers us tenderly; that God nurtures us, fosters us, feeds us; that God delights in us and wants us to flourish; that God is in our midst dancing for joy because of us.[1] Ultimately, it is the imagery of lover with beloved that comes closest to the mystery of God's quiet, abiding presence, as expressed in the wedding poetry of the Song of Songs: "I belong to my lover and for me he yearns" (Sg 7:11).

In silence we can sometimes sense this divine closeness, sometimes glimpse this place of unassailable intimacy. The poet Gerald Manley Hopkins alluded to it as the wellspring of "all this juice and all this joy" that arises annually in the abundant freshness of spring. John of the Cross described this corner of our hearts as an orchard that God passes through "in haste, leaving them by his glance alone, clothed in beauty."

Rainer Maria Rilke, the nineteenth-century German poet, surely felt the tender vigilance of the wake flame. In his *Book of Hours* he speaks to God as the nearest of neighbors, separated from us by nothing more than a flimsy wall of words that inevitably fall short of the Presence they attempt to name:

> You, neighbor God, if sometimes in the night
> I rouse you with loud knocking, I do so
> only because I seldom hear you breathe;
> and I know you are alone.
> And should you need a drink, no one is there
> to reach it to you, groping in the dark.
> Always I hearken. Give but a small sign.
> I am quite near.
> Between us there is but a narrow wall,
> and by sheer chance. For it would take

merely a call from your lips or from mine
to break it down. And that without a sound.
The wall is builded of your images.
They stand before you, hiding you like names.
And when the light within me blazes high
that in my inmost self I know you by,
the radiance is squandered on their frames.
And then my senses, which too soon grow lame,
exiled from you, must go their homeless ways.[2]

Those who experience the wake flame, even for a moment, can find their lives upended. They know it to be not only comfort and refuge and source of juice and joy, but also fiercely all-consuming, as only love can be. "Is not my word like fire," God asks, "like a hammer shattering rocks?" (Jer 23:29). This conviction of the wake flame has never since left me. I experience it sometimes as a warming presence in the dark, sometimes as a piercing laser revealing ways I am not yet truly loving, and at other times like a tiny blowtorch prodding me when I've become too settled down in the land. This constant, graced awareness of the wake flame serves as a kind of a spiritual "GPS," a touchstone for who and where I am and where I am going.

Shortly after my long retreat had finished, I went browsing in the poetry stacks of Kepler's Bookstore in Menlo Park, California, where the books are arranged alphabetically by author. With my head cocked sideways skimming the book spines looking for Rilke, my eyes chanced instead on the poet Rumi. The name stirred a dim memory. A Persian colleague at work had mentioned Rumi's name to me a year or so earlier, but I had been too busy to pursue it. I recalled only that Rumi was a Sufi—Sufism being a mystical branch of Islam more focused on interior prayer than on the external practice of religion—and that his poetry was still revered throughout the Middle East, many hundreds of years after his death.

Now, out of idle curiosity I picked up *Open Secret*, a slim paperback volume of Rumi's poems, and flipped casually through it. And right then and there, in the middle of that crowded shop, this prayer leapt off page seventy-four and loosed in me a sudden wild flood of tears:

The Music

For sixty years I have been forgetful
Every minute, but not for a second
Has this flowing toward me stopped or slowed.
I deserve nothing. Today I recognize
That I am the guest the mystics talk about.
I play this living music for my Host.
Everything today is for the Host.[3]

These words, penned by a thirteenth-century Persian, untranslated and mostly unknown in the West until recently, were describing my twenty-first-century spiritual life with uncanny precision. Not for a second has *this flowing toward me* stopped or slowed. Not for one second has God's attentiveness toward me waned.[4] Never mind that I am routinely forgetful of God's graciousness. Never mind that I often think my talents or accomplishments are my own doing, or that I live most of the time with the merest shreds of awareness. Not for a single moment has this wake flame disappeared. Not for a second has God forgotten me. Even more amazing: I am in fact the guest whom God constantly welcomes. Since this is true, what else could possibly matter?

In an instant the incredible *gratuity* of this undeserved welcome washed over me. It was, perhaps, what Buddhists might call a moment of enlightenment—suddenly understanding that the welcome I had been trying to extend to refugees all these years was not *my* doing, not *my* ministry. It wasn't about daily effort and straining and wearing myself out. My desire to live with a stance of welcome toward others was in reality the overflow, the excess, the inexplicable extravagance of God's unending welcoming of me. In fact, I am God's guest, every day and everywhere.

Now, you may think I exaggerate; but tears arising spontaneously do not deceive. The only possible response to a moment like this is stunned adoration—some sort of music or dance or poetry, some melting of life into praise and thanksgiving. It was already happening, right there in Kepler's poetry aisle. Not knowing or caring whether anyone stared, I spun into a corner and sat on a ledge with the book open on my lap, the tears flowing. I felt I was literally falling *into* the poem, into a sort of Alice-in-Wonderland hole in my heart, a tender place where my life did not at all resemble the pedestrian, competent, in-control self I presented to the world. Here, out of sight all these years even from myself; here, where the wake flame never wavered; here, where God donned an apron and prepared a feast and expectantly waited for my coming home; here, I suddenly found myself to be the guest that Rumi speaks of.

Tears kept coming, riding on unchecked joy. I suppose a silly grin washed across my face, too. I may even have looked drunk. But none of that mattered to me. As sometimes happens during intense spiritual experiences (after all, God is a God of joy and laughter), I remember having a completely random, humorous, ridiculous, fleeting thought, *What if the hokey-pokey* is *what it's all about?* and then laughing uncontrollably out loud. *No, it's all about the wake flame, stupid,* I gently chided myself as the moment passed. I was filled with a joy that I wanted to shout about from the rooftop!

Life isn't so much that we are seeking God (whether earnestly, sporadically, desperately, or not at all), but rather that God is already here with a steady lamp in the dark, searching for us. Life isn't how we stumble about trying to do no harm while we make occasional, feeble lurches at loving one another. Life is what God is doing within us and among us, nonstop—and it's not a death march, it's a dance. Life is about hearing this music and getting in step. Maybe the whirling dervishes (Rumi paramount among them) are on to something after all.

But, as Jack Kornfeld is fond of reminding spiritual seekers, after the ecstasy comes the laundry.[5] Though God remains attentive, I often do not seem capable of returning the favor. Even after repeated encounters of startling, slap-my-forehead immediacy when God seems deliriously close and I vow that my life will never, ever be the same again, I drift back into my usual fog of forgetfulness. One minute I am riveted by a sense of divine Presence—with every ounce of my being standing hushed on tiptoe while God is possibly passing by, the way all those little metal shavings in the children's game jump to vertical attention when the magnet hovers over them—and the next minute I am hunting for scissors to trim the hangnail that's suddenly bothering me.

Does this not seem surprising? It does to me. Despite moments of overpowering awareness of God's presence, I usually return to forgetfulness. I am living proof that haphazard, barely conscious existence trumps real awareness most of the time. It's as if I float absent-mindedly on the surface of familiar waters, dealing with the waves and the passing boats and the occasional fish that leap into my line of sight. All the while there is a tremendous surging of life beneath me, much too rich and varied and vibrant to imagine, from which every now and then I feel a tugging (in alternately delightful and disruptive ways) despite my stubborn preference for predictable surface sea and sun.

This is how it happens in my life; maybe you will catch variations of it in your own.

For a stretch of eight years, at the end of the work day on the last Monday of every month, I plopped into my car and headed 250 miles south from San Jose to Bakersfield. The purpose of my trip was to attend a board meeting early the next morning, after which I immediately began the trip in reverse. Most of the route was on Highway 5, a mind-numbingly straight furrow that slices through the farmlands of California's Central Valley. Ninety-six trips of 500 miles; 48,000 miles—nearly twice the circumference of the Earth. And even when clipping along at seventy miles per hour, I faced hours of monotonous cattle pastures, cotton fields, and almond orchards, interrupted only by occasional outcroppings dispensing food and fuel to weary travelers.

The weather in the valley is almost always hot, and sometimes hotter. Irrigation systems have salvaged the soil on both sides of the highway from what would otherwise be desert; but on windy days the tractors still churn up choking plumes of dust, and by night giant tumbleweeds bounce across the road, looming sudden and ghostly in the headlights as they carom off car bumpers. When tule fog hugs the ground, lending B-movie eeriness to the dark and shrinking visibility to a few miserable feet, drivers have no alternative but to pull over and wait until it decides to lift.

This was not my favorite commute.

I passed the time by listening to baseball on the radio, inventing psalms to sing, or scrambling the letters from passing license plates to form words. For the most part, however, the trip was unbearably dull. The endless dotted line on the asphalt induced only torpor. One such night, having at last turned drowsily eastward off the highway toward my destination, I noticed a nondescript building proclaiming itself to be "The Wide Awake Church of Life."

The what? My car had zipped past it so fast, I wasn't sure I had read it correctly. During the night I mulled it over. On my return drive the next day, I watched carefully for it. Sure enough, there it was—an ordinary sign in plain view just a few feet off the road, planted solidly next to the steps of a squat stucco building topped by a cross: The Wide Awake Church of Life.

Wow, I wondered. *What goes on in there? What might it take to qualify for membership?*

My thoughts stayed with that sign. *Why hadn't I seen it on any of my previous trips? Was I sleep-walking through life, the way I'd been nearly sleep-driving to Bakersfield? What had this sign triggered in me? How would ordinary things (and people) look if I were completely awake, really paying attention?*

Living in California had exposed me, of course, to plenty of New Age "being there" messages touting the significance of peeling an orange or focusing Zen-like on one's breathing. In no way, however, had

I gotten the point that paying attention just might be something God desired of me. Or that paying attention might change my life. But now, speeding north past cows and cotton, I wondered: *Was spirituality mostly about paying attention?* Something important was struggling toward consciousness, despite my usual distracted state. *What could this mean for my life?*

It was almost as if God had reached out and cradled my chin, turning my face toward that ever-patient Presence and saying, *"I'm* right here. Where are *you?"*

From some neglected corner of memory emerged the recollection of an art print that had hung in the office of the Sister who trained us as young postulants. At the time I had been more attracted by its colorful calligraphy than by its content:

> Keep me from going to sleep.
> Or if I go to sleep too soon:
> Come: Wake me up!
> Come any hour of the night.
> Make me look.
> See that I see.
> Talk to me till I am half as awake as You.[6]

I cannot recall the quotation's source—whether saint or poet or novice, it doesn't matter—but am impressed now by its urgent wisdom.

After this road trip epiphany, I began to see evidence everywhere that being spiritual was fundamentally about living each moment with direct, unfiltered awareness. It seemed obvious now—how had I not seen it earlier?—that the saints and gurus of all the religious traditions emphasized the absolute importance of paying attention. I was like a child beginning to read who suddenly notices alphabet letters at every turn and delights in deciphering them. Suddenly there were references everywhere that beckoned me to wake up and take notice lest, as Evelyn Underhill cautioned, "for lack of attention, a thousand forms of loveliness elude us every day."[7]

I remembered a wordless traffic sign that I had seen while visiting a dear friend in Aachen, Germany; posted at many of the intersections of the narrow cobblestone streets was an equilateral triangle with a dramatic exclamation point in the center. I suppose it was meant to caution drivers about blind corners, but for me it became a kind of private code: "Pay attention! God is passing by! Perhaps just around the corner here . . . ?" I copied the sign into my prayer journal.

I began to think of myself as an undercover agent for The Wide Awake Church of Life, secretly trying to home in on the present moment. Prior to this tectonic shift, my life had been almost entirely about the future. I had a compulsive work ethic. I excelled at making elaborate to-do lists and simultaneously juggling phones, e-mail, and visitors without blinking. The present moment was nowhere in my lifestyle. Even my brisk walk betrayed me; I was always moving full-speed ahead, cramming as much work as humanly possible into each hour.

Now, however, I began to understand what Etty Hillesum, a Jewish woman from Amsterdam, might have meant when she wrote in her journal during World War II:

> Before, I always lived in anticipation . . . [convinced] that it was all a preparation for something else, something "greater," more "genuine." But that feeling has dropped away from me completely. I live here and now, this minute, this day, to the full, and the life is worth living.[8]

Etty was not an overtly religious person, but she was a relentless seeker who honestly chronicled her experience. She found herself drawn to God almost despite herself, by some mysterious force that pushed her to her knees; from that position she tried to make space for something like God:

> Let this be the goal of meditation: to become like a wide open space, without that sneaky brushwood taking away your vista. That something like 'God' can enter, just like there is something of 'God' in the Ninth of Beethoven.[9]

She did it by paying attention, even as Hitler's occupying forces stripped away all normalcy, imposed ghetto restrictions, and ultimately shipped her to Auschwitz. "Get into touch with that little piece of eternity inside of you," she advised in September of 1941. Three months later she wrote that if she had to describe the whole year in one word, it would be "awakening." She who called herself a "kneeler in training" found meaning, strength, and enviable calm by focusing on the present moment—and implicitly, the God discovered there—even amid the horrors of a concentration camp:

> Be thanked, O Lord. In my inner dominions quietness and
> peace now rule. It really was a difficult journey. It now
> seems so simple and self-evident.[10]

From Nazi confinement Etty wrote that she desired to become balm for the wounds of others. Her brief, turbulent, beautiful life ended abruptly in Auschwitz at age twenty-nine.

Insights very similar, though originating in vastly different circumstances, come from the seventeenth-century monk known simply as Brother Lawrence, an unschooled man who spent his life washing pots and pans in a monastery kitchen. The title of his collected notes and conversations, *The Practice of the Presence of God*, communicates the focused awareness that gave rise to what observers described as his unwavering, radiant joy.

Such singular attentiveness does not mesh readily with my multitasking, flash-forward lifestyle. During my novitiate, I resisted mightily the convent counsel to devote my whole attention to one thing at a time (in order to achieve what was, in the devotion of that era, known as "the perfection of ordinary actions"). Au contraire. I took stubborn (though hidden, I hoped) pride in being able to do any number of things at once. Anything less would be wasting time—a peculiarly American sin. But after being broadsided by The Wide Awake Church of Life, that conviction crumbled. Time now held possibilities other than speed.

The familiar story of Moses and the Burning Bush seems different to me now. I had always liked this nifty account of Moses' vocation, his calling from God. The narrative has an engaging mix of characters (Moses tending his father-in-law's flocks, an angel appearing in flame, and God putting in a cameo appearance). It takes place in a vivid setting (the desert nomad herding his flock and coming upon the mysterious bush at the foot of Mount Horeb). It contains memorable dialogue (well, anytime God speaks directly to you, it's likely to be memorable). And it has a clever twist of plot (a bush that fire cannot reduce to ash).

I'd always assumed the point of the story was to be sure to listen when God calls your name, and perhaps that is the point; who can know for sure? But in my newly acquired, wait-a-minute-here, pay-attention mode, another angle arose: *How is it that Moses noticed that this bush was not being burnt up?* Think about this. Moses must have looked, really looked, at that bush for a long, long time before concluding that, whoa, it was not being consumed by the flames. Had he been passing by while, say, instant messaging on his iPhone or even reciting his daily prayers, he would surely have missed it. Well, he would have seen only a bush on fire—not an extraordinary sight. Scrub brush is burned every day in the desert for fuel. No, Moses was paying serious attention. The text notes that "as he looked on, Moses was surprised to see that the bush, though on fire, was not consumed" (Ex 3:2). Moses must have been gazing at that bush for a good long while before he realized something out-of-the-ordinary was happening. Only after this prolonged attentiveness did Moses hear God speak his name. He knew then that he was standing on holy ground. He took off his sandals and entered into conversation with the God whose Presence would completely change his life.

The contemporary poet David Whyte describes a parallel moment in his own life, when his eyes opened to the Holy Presence pulsing beneath his feet in the ordinary stuff of daily life:

Life is no passing memory of what has been
Nor the remaining pages in a great book waiting to be
    read.
It is the opening of eyes long closed.
It is the vision of far-off things seen for the silence they
    hold.
It is the heart, after years of secret conversing, speaking
    out,
Loud in the clear air.
It is Moses in the desert, fallen to his knees before the lit
    bush.
It is the man throwing away his shoes as if to enter heaven
And finding himself astonished
Opened at last,
Fallen in love with solid ground.[11]

Whyte says that real living is about neither memories preserved nor a future waiting to unfold. Rather, it is about awakening—"the opening of eyes long closed"—to what is immediately present. Like the astonished Moses who removes his sandals at the realization of God's nearness, Whyte understands that God is not located in some far-off celestial abode but is met in the embrace of daily life; that spirituality is, quite simply, about vulnerability and openness and falling in love with solid ground.

· Both poets and refugees have led me along this great adventure of waking up. Stephen Mitchell describes prayer as "a quality of attention" that makes "so much room for the given, that it can appear as gift."[12] In other words, when we look with gentle regard upon whatever is right before our eyes—whatever the *givens* are in our lives, without denying or negating anything—we gradually learn to see that it is all *gift* to be treasured. The etymology makes it obvious: Givens are gifts. How to maintain that elusive attentiveness to the present moment, however, is far from obvious. I do know one thing: In the brief snatches of time when I recognize whatever life is throwing at me as *gift* and can manage a stammered *thank you*, I am at my happiest. It is simply impossible to be both grateful and unhappy at the same time.[13]

Like Rumi, I have to admit that for sixty years I have been forgetful, mostly absent from life, mostly going about occupied with "matters of consequence."[14] Refugees, on the other hand—perhaps because their useful livelihood has been so wrenchingly taken from them—seem much more able to dwell in the present tense.

In the busy center where I welcomed and resettled refugees from many countries, there were constant comings and goings, and I was usually racing from one meeting or deadline to the next. One day Kwot, a tall, rather dignified-looking man from southern Sudan, asked to see me. "Sure," I said, ushering him to a chair in my office. "I suppose you're here about the loan we arranged . . . ," and then I blathered on for several minutes about the payment details. All the while Kwot sat there, saying not one word. Finally, I realized I was doing all the talking. I brought the monologue to an embarrassed halt. Kwot still said nothing; he just looked at me. Then he smiled and said, "Sister: *Hello.*" After another polite pause, he said that he had not come about the loan. He didn't want anything at all, other than to bring me his greetings because he had not seen me for a while. He was apologizing for not having paid attention to me for a few weeks. I immediately shrank to the size of a brussels sprout.

Another young refugee whom we resettled, a French-speaking survivor of torture from Cameroon, stopped by my office quite often. His walk was so graceful and light that I never heard him coming down the hallway. Rather, I'd *feel* his presence, turn around, and see him standing as motionless in the doorway as an apparition. He'd beam a smile at me and say in his careful, newly acquired English, "I come to greet you!" And that was *all* he wanted—simply to greet me. Like an angel of annunciation. He might as well have said, "Take off your shoes; this is holy ground."

These refugees—and so many others like them—know the importance of being present, really present, wherever they are. They tend relationships (like precious wake flames) because that is all they have. Everything else has been lost in war and upheaval and flight and long, "useless" years in the limbo of foreign camps. They are starting life over now in a new land, without family, without possessions, without money, without even a sense of where they belong anymore in the world, and often without the language to express to new companions either their bewilderments or their hopes. So they pay careful attention to whatever presents itself to them, right here, right now—this flowing toward them, however strange.

Whatever we pay attention to *grows*. The poet May Sarton contends that if we look with tender care at almost anything—a stone, the bark of a tree, grass, a cloud—something akin to revelation occurs. Something is "given," she says, "and perhaps that something is always a reality *outside* the self."[15] Andrew Harvey, a Rumi scholar, hints at the unveiling that awaits us when we slow down and pay attention. We are likely to be undone by the enormity of the revelation.

> As the seeker deepens her experience . . . an astounding secret starts to derange her—she realizes that what she has read in the great mystical books of every tradition is not poetry or enthusiastic exaggeration, but a literal and all-shattering truth: that she and the Beloved are not separate but one and that the One she is looking for is also looking for her. . . . [T]hat everything is held together by the force of love, that every atom is drunk on this love, and that the universe that before seemed so orderly is in fact always reeling in drunken, ecstatic dance.[16]

It's the burning bush all over again. It's giddy revelation at Kepler's. It's The Wide Awake Church of Life. And there is nothing sentimental about it. It's an unexpected, undeserved, loving Presence flowing toward us, sweeping us all up in a grand, crazy waltz (or hip-hop or tango!) with everyone and everything. It's the divine Host literally turning the tables to prepare a banquet for us. And we realize, to our unending astonishment, that we're *all* invited guests.

STRANGER *God*

One evening not long after 9/11, I received a voicemail message from Daniel, a Sudanese refugee whom my Catholic Charities colleagues and I had resettled in San Jose. Daniel is a soft-spoken young man in his twenties, one of the "Lost Boys" of Sudan who spent twelve years in East African refugee camps prior to coming to the United States. We had since become friends.

Daniel's voice on my answering machine sounded tight with worry: "Please, Sister, call me."

When I phoned him back, we exchanged pleasantries for a good while, as is the custom in African culture, and then I asked him why he had contacted me.

"I will be going to hospital tomorrow."

"Yes," I said. I knew that he would be having an appendectomy. I asked if he was worried about the operation, his first in an American hospital.

"No, that's not the problem."

"Hmmm," I said. "Something else is bothering you?"

"Well, yes," he answered, paused, and then added with the solemnity of a bailiff parsing out a death sentence, "the doctors told me that when I come in tomorrow, they will ask me to sign on a paper *whether I want to donate my heart to them.*"

He paused again, swallowed hard, and then blurted out, "Sister, why would I want to donate my heart to a stranger?"

As you can imagine, Daniel was relieved to learn about the voluntary nature of organ donation and that no one in the medical profession would be pestering him to give up his heart while he was still alive. But the question he posed still tugs at my heart. It seems to me a profoundly important question, one we all might well consider—especially now, when our world is full of strangers and our natural instinct is to protect ourselves from them. Why would I want to give my heart to a stranger? Because God shows an unnerving proclivity for showing up in the stranger's guise. This has enormous implications, not only for our efforts to assist and advocate for refugees, but for the current debate about immigration.

Everyone has an opinion about migrants, about problems along borders, about the benefits or limits of diversity, about the complex consequences of the population shifts that are quite literally changing the face of the northern hemisphere. We worry about safeguarding our standard of living and about protecting ourselves from "outsiders" (whom some media and even government voices would have us equate with "terrorists"). Politicians and talk-show hosts intentionally tap into the very real fears we have about strangers in our midst.

The word *stranger*, after all, means someone unknown, someone alien, "other," not like us. We tell children not to talk to strangers. We lock our doors against them. Strangers are persons who stand outside of our group; by definition, they are people who don't belong. Their presence among us stirs anxiety.

A quarter-century prior to 9/11, Dutch spiritual author Henri Nouwen wrote, "People who are unfamiliar, speak another language, have another color, wear a different type of clothes, and live a lifestyle different from ours make us afraid and even hostile. In our world, the assumption is that strangers are a potential danger."[1] In today's world, those fears have magnified to the point where homeland security measures now outrank constitutional safeguards.

We should be amazed, then—and frankly, disturbed—by the significance of strangers in the Judeo-Christian scriptures. It surprises most people (the majority of Christians included) to learn that the second most frequently repeated mandate in those scriptures is to welcome strangers and treat them kindly.[2] This appears, in one form or another, three dozen times in the Torah alone and sixty-seven additional places throughout the Bible.

In Hebrew scripture, God voices extraordinary concern for three categories of persons: widows, orphans, and aliens. Understanding the need to protect widows and orphans is not too challenging; they are often kin, they are in obvious need, and they are so vulnerable that surely they pose no threat. But strangers? Aliens? Apparently, from God's perspective, offering hospitality to them, sharing what one has with them, is a matter of utmost consequence. Further, God views this as a matter of justice. It's about doing what is right and what is expected of us by God, not about giving handouts from a comfortable surplus. It costs. Its economic implications are spelled out in practical terms, as when God speaks in the Book of Leviticus to land owners:

> When you reap the harvest of your land, you shall not be so thorough that you reap the field to its very edge, nor shall you glean the stray ears of your grain. These things you shall leave for the poor and the alien. I, the LORD, am your God. (Lv 23:22)

Furthermore, every third year the tithing portion of the harvest was to be given not to the temple but to the poor:

> At the end of every third year you shall bring out all the tithes of your produce for that year and deposit them in community stores, that the Levite who has no share in the heritage with you, and also the alien, the orphan and the widow who belong to your community, may come and eat

their fill; so that the LORD, your God, may bless you in all
that you undertake. (Dt 14:23, 28–29)

Hospitality to strangers figured prominently in biblical cultures.
The Hebrew people knew from their own history what it meant to
be exiles, wayfarers depending on the kindness of others. Conse-
quently, reciprocal kindness was woven into their moral code. Not
that it was easy! Perhaps that's why the command appears so often—
to remind us, to goad us, to impress upon us that this is how God
acts, so this is how we must act:

> For the LORD, your God . . . mighty and awesome . . . has no
> favorites, accepts no bribes . . .executes justice for the orphan
> and the widow, and befriends the alien, feeding and clothing
> him. So you too must befriend the alien, for you were once
> aliens yourselves in the land of Egypt. (Dt 10:17–20)

> When an alien resides with you in your land, do not molest
> him. You shall treat the alien who resides with you no differ-
> ently than the natives born among you; have the same love for
> him as for yourself; for you too were once aliens in the land of
> Egypt. I, the LORD, am your God. (Lv 19:33–34)

The practice of offering hospitality to strangers wasn't merely an
obedient response to a command. It evolved out of the lived experience of the Jewish people: Extending welcome to the strangers in
their midst was literally seen as one way of meeting God.[3] Creating
space for strangers, inviting them into one's own circle of friends and
family—this was a concrete way of encountering the Holy One.

The poet D.H. Lawrence, while acknowledging that fear is our
normal response to strangers, hints that blessings await those who risk
opening their door to the stranger's knock:

> What is the knocking?
> What is the knocking at the door in the night?
> It is somebody wants to do us harm.
> No, no, it is the three strange angels.
> Admit them. Admit them.[4]

The poet was alluding to the intriguing story narrated in the book of Genesis, chapter 18. In this incident Abraham sees three strangers at a distance, walking along. He dashes after them, calling out and begging them not to walk on past his tent, but instead to come and receive his hospitality. The writer notes that Abraham (notwithstanding his status as an elder) literally bows down to the ground before these strangers. He pleads with them: "Please, come be refreshed and enjoy a meal with us." As the story unfolds, it turns out that these three men are actually messengers of God. In the ensuing conversation they reveal that Abraham's elderly wife Sarah will no longer remain barren, but will bear them a son who will in turn found a great nation. It couldn't be more plain, really—an act of hospitality to the stranger plays a key role in the founding of the people of Israel.

Hospitality is so culturally important to Abraham that, even though these three strangers had not asked for rest or water or assistance, Abraham is appalled by the prospect that they might simply walk past his tent without stopping. He has to jump up, flag them down, cajole them into staying: "Please, this matters to me! You must become my guests. Do me this favor! It would be an insult if you did not allow me to share all that I have with you. Seat yourselves right here in the shade. Stay awhile. Let my servants prepare a meal for you. . . ." Centuries later, reflecting on this story, the author of the Letter to the Hebrews wrote to the first-generation Christians, "Do not neglect hospitality, for through it some have unknowingly entertained angels" (Heb 13:2).

There is a similarly surprising story in the first book of Kings, chapter 17. Here we find a widow from the town of Zarephath on the verge of death as she collects bits of firewood to cook some few scraps of food for her starving son and herself. The prophet Elijah appears (of course, to the widow he is only a complete stranger with really bad timing), asking for food and drink. Though she has almost no food and tells the stranger that he is imposing on them, she nevertheless provides him the requested meal. The grateful Elijah, in turn, sees to it that her jug of oil will never run dry nor her jar of flour ever be empty through all the ensuing years of drought and famine ravaging that land.

A pattern emerges here: In the scriptures the stranger is not simply someone who needs our hospitality; the stranger is the one who actually *brings us blessings*. If we have eyes to see, the roles of giver and receiver reverse and the stranger reveals the divine presence to us. In the person of the other, the alien, we may meet the God who is always "other," always beyond what we can think or imagine. And if we are open to such encounters, there is the chance for unexpected blessings. Speaking of God, St. John of the Cross wrote, "He passed through these groves in haste, scattering a thousand blessings, and left them, by his glance alone, clothed in beauty."[5] In my experience, this is what God is *always* doing—passing through our lives, scattering blessings— but in our busyness we rarely stop long enough to notice them, to cherish them, or to give thanks for them.

Blessings are God's constant outflowings of love, attracting us and in the process making us attractive. Blessings are the presence of God flowing into us and through us, uniting us with one another and all creation. The effect of blessing is always to bring together, to reconcile, to unite, to enable us to see people as their best selves (namely, as beloved of God). And when we know ourselves to be blessed, then we in turn can bless others. William Butler Yeats describes his own astonishment at being sideswiped by precisely such an unanticipated experience of blessing:

> My fiftieth year had come and gone.
> I sat a solitary man in a crowded London shop,
> An open book and empty cup on the marble tabletop.
> While on the shop and street I gazed
> My body of a sudden blazed.
> For twenty minutes, more or less,
> It seemed so great, my happiness,
> That I was blessed, and could bless.[6]

Yeats' poem describes the ordinariness of a middle-aged person sitting at a street-side cafe—a rather unpromising spot for a sudden experience of the holy. Yet who among us hasn't had such moments? Often coming when we seem least ready, God does suddenly seem close to us, and that felt closeness releases a surge of joy—joy not to be savored as a private treasure, but joy that spills outward as blessing for others.

In such moments there are no strangers. We know, really know in our very bones, that every person is brother and sister. This is true community, what theologians call the "communion of saints," the reality that all of us are inextricably connected. Poets say it best: "In the shade of the cherry blossom tree, there are no strangers."[7] Because we ourselves are blessed, we discover that we can become a blessing for others.

In Nong Khai refugee camp, 14,000 persons lived in unnaturally crowded conditions, allotted a mere eighteen inches of living space per person. I learned a great deal there about hospitality and about blessing. When it came time for the new year, I asked one of the young men how the Lao people traditionally celebrated the holiday.[8] I will never forget his response: "Oh, we go from house to house saying blessings." How different the world might be if we all spent some time going from house to house, from person to person, spreading blessings.

To mark life's transitions (births, weddings, comings and goings) the Lao people always have a *baci*—a ceremony wherein the honored guest sits next to a bouquet of elegantly arranged flowers from which hang thin white strings. One by one, each person at the celebration comes up to the honoree, kneels down in front of him/her, takes a string from the bouquet, and ties it around the person's wrist while speaking a spontaneous blessing. The strings remain on the person's wrist for the next three days as a sign of blessings being carried, a remembrance of who bestowed them, and evidence that we are all "tied" to one another.

What about the opposite of blessing? The curse. The very word has an old-fashioned ring to it, evoking images of a villain who slinks off-stage muttering, "Curses! Foiled again!" Its root meaning is to cut off, to excommunicate. Of course, we don't go around excommunicating people anymore. Or do we? Whenever we cut other persons off from us or from the community, treat them as unwelcome for any reason, we are *de facto* excommunicating them. Cursing them. Anytime we set boundaries and declare that certain others must stay on the far side, we are cursing. Anytime we choose to divide "them" from "us," we are cursing, stifling the life-breath of God, that Spirit whose movement is always toward reconciliation and unity.

The scriptures call us to keep on blessing, to keep on extending the circle of our concern until no one is left outside, no one is a stranger any longer. The dominant voices in our world today tell us what a foolhardy stance that is, and that we should instead "circle our wagons," protecting what we have from those who have less. One way of measuring whether our love is genuine, however, is to examine how far we've extended the boundaries that determine whom we are willing to be in relationship with. When these borders reach out as far as they can go, there will be no one left outside, there will be no one cursed. There will be no more strangers. Everyone will be welcome.

Reflect for a minute on what it feels like to be *welcomed*. The word means, simply, "come and be well" in my presence. It's a fundamental human experience, and a very crucial one. When I am welcomed, I feel good. I can be myself. I relax and feel unself-conscious, energized, happy. On the other hand, when I am *not* welcomed, I doubt myself, turn inward, shrivel up. I feel excluded, not accepted, and not acceptable. This is painful. If it happens often enough, I will question my own self-worth.

Hospitality means creating welcoming space for the other. Henri Nouwen notes that the Dutch word for hospitality, *gastvrijheid*, means "the freedom of the guest."[9] It entails creating not just physical room but emotional spaciousness where the stranger can enter and be himself or herself, where the stranger can become ally instead of threat, friend instead of enemy.

God does that. God is forever welcoming us, creating space for us, allowing us to be who we really are. That precious experience—when contemplated, cherished, and celebrated—enables me in turn to welcome others: I begin to be less fearful of the other; I start to see the stranger as gift. I become willing to create space in myself to invite the other in, and I open myself to the possibility of being changed by the presence of the other.

I invite the reader to sit with any of the wonderful hospitality stories found in the traditions of all the great religions. Mull them over; ask God for insight into them. Then ask for courage to take small steps in expanding your own circle of hospitality. These might be as tentative as smiling at the stranger in line with you at the grocery store, as deliberate as hosting a get-together for all the strangers in your apartment building, or as dramatic as volunteering to foster an unaccompanied refugee child in your own home. It might not cost you much, or it might mean going out on a limb: Can you imagine yourself during Thanksgiving dinner speaking up to your brother-in-law in defense of the undocumented, pointing out that, really, everyone is kin to us, and everyone has a human right to live where they can support their own family?

An ancient proverb describes Abraham's tent as being "open on all four sides." It's a gracious image, worth pondering. How open are we "on all sides" to being surprised by the strangers whom we encounter? How willing are we to invite them in? *Tent*, of course, is an English word; the Latin equivalent is *tabernaculum*—holy dwelling place of God on earth.

Other cultures can teach us about hospitality. You may be familiar with the Western proverb: "After three days, fish and houseguests stink." In Africa the proverb says, "After three days, your guest becomes your brother." In Afghanistan the saying is even more challenging: "With the first cup of tea you are my guest; with the second

175

you become my friend; and with the third you are part of my family."
Which cultures seem closer to God's way of viewing the world?

David Steindl-Rast, Benedictine monk and author, says that the
truest name for God is "Surprise!" because all other names must eventually fall short. We can never grasp God or fully understand who God
is; the mystery remains beyond grasping. God is always more than we
can fathom. God is always "other." This theme appears even in Homer's ancient epic poem, *The Odyssey*:

> For gods may wear the guise of strangers come from far-off
> lands; they take on many forms and roam about the cities;
> they would see if men live justly or outrageously.[10]

From the very earliest stories of Judeo-Christian faith, God has
appeared as the stranger. Why should it be any different today? Welcome a stranger into your tent; it may become a tabernacle.

The scriptural mandate to welcome strangers looms large in the
life and teachings of Jesus. During his life, Jesus experienced himself as an outsider. In one of the infancy narratives, there is no room
for him at the inn when he is born (Lk 2:7). In another, he is forced
to flee into another land to avoid being butchered by a mad tyrant.
When he begins his preaching, he is thrown out of his own syna-
gogue and nearly tossed off a cliff, vehemently rejected by his own
townspeople (Lk 4:14–30). He remains a stranger even to his own
relatives, who think he has gone mad (Lk 9:58). He admits that he
has "nowhere to lay his head"(Mt 8:20). And, ultimately, he dies the
type of death, crucifixion, reserved by the Romans only for aliens.
As the author of the letter to the Hebrews points out, "He died outside the gate"(Heb 13:12). John's Gospel sums it up in one poignant
line, "He came to what was his own, but his own people did not ac-
cept him"(Jn 1:11).

Out of Jesus' own experience of being *not* welcome—and surely
he must have felt it keenly—he teaches his followers a radically different reality. His parables depict the amazing, unexpected, unconditional

welcome that is God's constant stance toward us, and he then challenges us to extend that same welcome to others.

The Parable of the Prodigal Son is really about the profound welcome that the father, who has long been keeping anxious vigil, extends to his wayward son. This elder runs down the road to wrap his son in a forgiving embrace before the son can even stammer the apology he's been rehearsing. The father escorts him into their home for a joyful, no-questions-asked reunion complete with an over-the-top party. Underscoring the lavishness of this scene, Jesus adds a description of the dutiful older brother's resentment. Despite having lived all his life under the same roof with this loving father, the older son still cannot comprehend the extravagance shown in welcoming home the prodigal. And, sadder still, the older brother completely misses the unbounded generosity (already given to both sons) revealed by the Father's baffled comment, "Don't you realize that everything I have is yours?"

To emphasize that such profound welcome is not limited only to kin, Jesus tells the scandalous parable of the Good Samaritan, a story so familiar that it has become a cliché in our culture despite nearly disappearing from our practice. We've heard it so many times. To our ears the story line sounds tame. We miss the deliberate shock value of its original telling.

Samaritans qualified as strangers, yes—but much worse, they were apostates, enemies of the true faith. Any contact with a Samaritan rendered a Jew unclean. Perhaps today we should rename the protagonist the Good Terrorist, the Good Illegal, or even the Good Pedophile. It isn't the believer in God who is reaching out to the injured foreigner, but rather the reverse.

The despised alien Samaritan befriends the good Jewish believer. He inconveniences himself, gets his hands dirty binding up the man's wounds, trudges on foot while the wounded man rides on his donkey, and finally—as if he hadn't already done enough—uses his own money to pay for the man's continued lodging and care. With no limits! "Do whatever is needed for him," the Samaritan instructs the innkeeper, "and I will cover the costs when I return." Who among us would write a blank check like that for a complete stranger who was half-dead anyway? Yet this is literally what the Samaritan does for his political and religious enemy. Jesus concludes the story with the blunt message, "Go and do the same." Not as a burdensome command, but as the secret to having fullness of life![11] Jesus' listeners—accustomed as they were to religion being about a code of purity spelled out in laws and rituals—must have been stunned; perhaps some walked away shaking their heads and muttering, "What kind of idiocy is this?"

Then there is the Parable of the Last Judgment. We know this story almost by heart. Jesus makes it painfully clear that what will matter at the time of our death is not our churchgoing, not our attainment of virtue, not our saying of prayers, not our donations to church coffers, not even our hard work. None of that. Rather, God will be looking for the simple acts of kindness that we extended to the hungry, the thirsty, the naked, *the stranger*, those who were least on our list. Why? Because that is where God was waiting all along, ready to engage with us. The least among us were our chance (perhaps our only chance) to demonstrate our love for God.

I recently watched a comedian on television describing how he walked past a homeless person on the street. Striding across the stage, microphone in hand, he acted out how he had looked back over his shoulder at the disheveled figure on the sidewalk, stopped a minute, and then backtracked to give the man a few coins. "Well, y'know," said the comedian in an aside, "I'm thinking, just maybe, there's the off-chance he *could* be Jesus!" The audience laughed. The comedian then bent over toward the invisible figure and stage-whispered, "Hey, pssst: I know who you *really* are." The audience laughed again, this time somewhat nervously.

The message hits home, even if we try to sidestep its implications: God waits to meet each of us precisely at our borders, outside our gates, at the edges of our lives, where "the least" dwell or are kept at arm's length. Thomas Merton described this uninvited, inconvenient God:

Into this world, this demented inn, in which there is absolutely no room for him at all, Christ has come uninvited. . . .
[H]is place is with those others for whom there is no room.
His place is with those who do not belong . . . who are dis-
credited, who are denied the status of persons. With those for
whom there is no room, Christ is present in the world. He
is mysteriously present in those for whom there seems to be
nothing but the world at its worst. It is in these that he hides
himself, for whom there is no room.[12]

So what are we to do?

The early Church struggled mightily with this question. Jesus was
the Messiah, yes—but just for the Jewish people, right? Even after Peter had dreamed a compelling vision of God's love encompassing all of
creation, it took the feistiness of Paul to face down the other disciples
at the Council of Jerusalem and insist that God does not limit God's
presence to the chosen few. God welcomes *all*. Everyone belongs inside the gates.

It's not an easy message to swallow. Paul's letters repeatedly insist
on inclusion, on reconciliation, on breaking down the barriers that
separate human beings one from another. As he wrote in Galatians
3:28, "There exists no more slave or free, Jew or Greek, male or fe-
male . . . All are *one* in Christ."

Paul's brief letter to his contemporary, Philemon, for example, is
a stunning challenge to the accepted social order. In it, Paul urges the
wealthy Philemon to welcome back Philemon's former slave, Onesimus. Paul knew full well that Onesimus had escaped from Philemon
and been guilty of theft in the process. Paul later converted the run-
away to Christianity. He tells Philemon to take Onesimus back into his
household as a brother in the Lord. Paul cagily suggests that Philemon
should allow Onesimus into the community of Christians at Colossae,
forgiving everything and taking him back *not as a slave but as a brother*!
"Welcome him as you would me," writes Paul. This was guaranteed to
upset just about everyone at Colossae—except, of course, the slaves.

It would be as if Paul wrote in our day to the US Border Patrol, asking them to welcome the undocumented aliens at the border as their brothers and sisters and to make room for them in their own homes. And then, just to add extra punch to the request, Paul coyly hints that he will be visiting Philemon shortly. "Get a room ready for me," Paul writes, perhaps to check on the extent of Philemon's hospitality to his former-slave-now-brother-in-the-Lord.

The early Christians took these teachings of Jesus seriously. They wrestled with the implications and struggled to change their lives accordingly. One hundred years after the life of Jesus, Aristides, a non-Christian, chronicled for the Emperor Hadrian in Rome his impression of Jesus' followers:

> Christians love one another. They never fail to help widows; they save orphans from those who would hurt them. If a man has something, he gives freely to the one who has nothing. *If they see a stranger, Christians take him home and are happy, as though he were a real brother.* They don't consider themselves brothers in the usual sense, but brothers instead through the Spirit, in God. . . . This is really a new kind of person. There is something divine in them.[13]

It's as revolutionary as it sounds.

A colleague was once giving a presentation in a local church regarding immigration policy in the context of Christian faith. During the talk a man in the audience raised his hand, stood up, and said, "I am sick and tired of being told to love my neighbor!" Blunt, but refreshingly honest. How much does God expect of us? Are each and every one of us responsible for confronting the injustices in our troubled world? And if so, how can God ask this of us and then have the nerve to proclaim, "My yoke is easy, my burden light"?

The answer lies in the graciousness of our God, who never issues a call without also extending a gift. In other words, along with every "hard saying" or prophetic challenge there is also given the grace to live that way, joyfully. In the words of Bill Spohn, late professor of ethics at Santa Clara University, "The call without the gift would be burdensome, oppressive. But the gift without the call would be mere pietism."[14] God lures us into goodness; God never shoves.

The invitation to conversion always includes the strength for conversion. Those who know God, who have been changed by God, are not dour people; in my experience, they are profoundly joyful. They have nothing to lose. They live in the freedom of Paul's counsel to Titus giving up everything that does not lead to God (Ti 2:12). Their tents are open on all sides. They personify welcome.

God is always and everywhere inviting us to such conversion. The call is toward an ever greater expansiveness that does away with distinctions and barriers. This might mean accepting a hidden part of myself that I have never been comfortable with or a co-worker whose idiosyncrasies test my patience. It could involve making space for an estranged member of family or community. Or it might mean reaching out to befriend a refugee newly arrived or an immigrant needing a job. It surely means viewing those who are "other" as revelation rather than threat. The movement of God's Spirit inclines us toward more and more inclusiveness. This is God's way of *justice* in the biblical sense of holiness and right relationships, not in the narrow American sense of fairness and equality.

The Gospel taken seriously tends to subvert the careful ordering of our lives. As Annie Dillard wrote, "It is madness to wear ladies' straw hats . . . to church; we should all be wearing crash helmets. Ushers should issue life preservers and signal flares; they should lash us to our pews."[15] Only a fool would think God's unconditional and constantly repeated welcome of us comes without the responsibility for us to go and do likewise.

The Gospel should startle us, cause us to cling to our pews in terror, and then knead our hearts until we are emboldened to work toward a world dangerously different from the status quo. The poor and marginalized, though we distance ourselves from them, are with us always—annoyingly, "like gum stuck to the shoes of the rich."[16] Our task is to create a world where these anonymous, disposable, impoverished sectors of humanity will finally be given places of respect. Those whom society calls illegal aliens, for example, and refugees, the homeless, the mentally ill, the desperately poor, those who have no friends or are of no account in the eyes of the world—these apparently are the very ones God is identifying most closely with: "I was a stranger and you welcomed me."

If we take seriously the life and message of Jesus, then we cannot avoid its uncomfortable consequence: God is the ultimate "other." God is coming today in the presence of unrecognized, unimportant "others," and our abiding happiness depends precisely upon meeting and welcoming and honoring in them this stranger God.

In my own interaction with refugees, I have experienced a God who sits with the abandoned, who weeps with the sorrowing, who encourages those on the verge of losing all hope. I know the God who walks—no, *limps* with the poor. I have met this God in refugees who share their meager rations of water with passers-by. I have heard God in the songs they sing into the desert night. I have stood beside God at graveside vigils for those who died of a scorpion bite or malaria. I have seen God in the eyes of child soldiers convinced that their deeds are unforgivable.

Sadly, this God might not be immediately recognizable by theologians looking for an All-Powerful Being or an Unmoved Mover. This God lives in "hiddenness" and seeks the lowest place. This God knows helplessness and sorrow and collects the tears of those who grieve. This God is all too familiar with neglect and confinement and failure. This God stands solidly against injustice, yet refuses all forms of violence. This God's face is mercy.

People sometimes ask me how I can continue to work with refugees year after year and not grow discouraged or heavily burdened. The question always surprises me. How could encountering God face-to-face be disheartening? Where else could I hope to find such blessing?

The truth is that in the very thick of it all—in the songs that rise from dry, dusty refugee camps; in the hearts of those who have survived torture; in the forging of new friendships; in the small miracles of life that stare down death—there lives, in Gerald Manley Hopkins' lovely phrase, "the dearest, freshness, deep-down things."[17] There lives the God of our hearts, the One who breaks down the "barriers of hostility"[18] that divide our troubled world. Despite the violence and poverty, the losses and the suffering and the insurmountable problems, God is present—the steady wake flame that can never be quenched.

This same God, of course, also sets the heavens spinning. Dances inside van Gogh's brush. Delights in the music of Taize, the poetry of Rumi, and the laughter of children. Answers to names like Wonderful, Counselor, Friend and Beloved, Desire of the Everlasting Hills, the One who is always there. Shelters with inexplicable tenderness all who draw near, and is endlessly inventive in wooing back those who stray. Once this God has our attention, however, we no longer have excuses for luke-warmness or delay. This God desires our hearts, yes, with a fierce desire, but first wants them connected "with leading strings of love" to the whole human family, especially the poor and outcast.

Like my friend Daniel, we must at some point confront the question, *Why would I donate my heart to a stranger?* There is only one possible reason: because God does. Because in the giving, we are drawn into God's strange and extravagant way of being. Because in that newfound intimacy we are pulled beyond our own preoccupations and into unexpected connectedness not only with widows and orphans, but also with aliens.

Imagine how different our world could be if we developed immigration policies based on the premise that keeping people out is not as crucial as establishing relationships with them. That our national security would be enhanced not by killing enemies but by making friends. That mortal dangers breed more readily in isolation than in global connectedness. That donating our hearts to strangers might bring us blessings more often than threats.

Imagine how different our world could be if we opened doors in the reckless hope that the unknown outsider standing a bit beyond our threshold of comfort just might be the Holy One for whom our hearts long.

MERCY AND JUSTICE SHALL KISS

During my first few months in Nong Khai refugee camp, I made a valiant but ultimately fruitless effort to master the Lao language. The grammar was not overly complex, and the graceful, squiggly alphabet not too difficult. I memorized its eighty-six letters and various accent marks, learned many vocabulary words, and became fairly proficient in copying the script by hand. Its pronunciation, however, completely stymied me. I simply could not distinguish the differing tones. As with many Asian languages, it really matters whether a Lao word is pronounced in a rising tone, a falling tone, an even tone, a high tone, or a low tone.

Moo, for example, means "friend"; but *moo* (sounds the same to me) means "pig." *Bah* means "aunt," but, with a subtle (I didn't hear it) shift, *bah* means "fish." *Gie* means "near"; *gie* means "far" (how can this be?)—and, oh yes, *gie* also means "chicken."

One day I was carefully sounding out a story from the Lao First Grade Primer about an eight-foot-long tiger chasing a boy through the

185

forest. Several refugees were listening politely, but their attentiveness quickly turned to sideways glances, then smirks and laughter.

"What's so amusing?" I asked.

"Well, there's just something funny about being chased through the forest by an eight-foot-long shirt!"

That's how I learned that *seuah* means "shirt," whereas *seuah* means "tiger"; and by the way, *seuah* means "mattress." It was all the same to my poor American ears. Sigh. It seemed pointless and even a bit dicey to speak even the simplest sentences:

> I want to give a pig/friend to my friend/pig.
> My aunt/fish lives far/chicken/near from here.
> My fish/aunt is friendly/piggish.
> I sleep on a mattress/tiger/shirt in my shirt/tiger/
>   mattress.

And that was just the first page of the book.

Nevertheless, early each morning my faithful tutor, Syda, would spend twenty minutes with me while I practiced reading aloud. His English was quite good, so whenever I couldn't decipher the meaning of the Lao vocabulary, he would explain it to me. One day, however, we came across a new word, *mehdtah,* that I just couldn't get. Syda did not know the English equivalent. He grasped for ways to explain it without success, and finally looked at me and said with deep feeling, "It's *what you are* for me and my family! Yes, it's exactly what *you* are." Intrigued, I made a note to pursue it further when I got back to the convent.

That night I searched for *mehdtah* in my pocket dictionary, and when I saw its meaning—*mercy*—tears rolled down my cheeks. Syda, of course, had no way of knowing that I am a Sister of Mercy. It was the greatest compliment he could have given me.

I have spent many years trying to align my life with the God of mercy, trying to become more compassionate, more attentive to suffering. Trying to be a better listener, someone who notices and responds to the burdens of others. Of course, I am a slow learner. I fail regularly and spectacularly, but there have been some rare, wonderful moments—as Syda's casual comment revealed—when *mehdtah* rises up, refusing to stay buried beneath my busyness.

The refugees taught me *mehdtah*.

In one of the resurrection stories in John's Gospel, Thomas (the famous doubter) says to the others who claim to have seen Jesus alive after the crucifixion, "Unless I see the mark of the nails in his hands and put my finger into the nailmarks and put my hand into his side, I will not believe" (Jn 20:25). There is grief beneath Thomas's stubbornness, certainly—he does not want to risk getting his hopes up, only to be dashed again—but there is also insight. Real belief in God comes only when encountering great human suffering face to face, coming dangerously close to it, touching it with one's own hands and heart. When we insulate ourselves from suffering, we also insulate ourselves from life and the kind of hope not defeated by death. We can meet the God who chooses to be close to the poor only when we choose to stand close to the poor, unshielded from their wounds and their heartbreak.

The Indian mystic and author Rabindranath Tagore, in *The Fugitive and Other Poems*, tells this Hindu story:

> The day came for the image from the temple to be drawn around the town in its chariot. The Queen said to the King, "Let us go and attend the festival."
>
> Only one man out of the whole household did not join in the pilgrimage. His work was to collect stalks of speargrass to make brooms for the King's house. The chief of the servants said in pity to him, "You may come with us."
>
> But he bowed his head, saying, "No, thank you, it cannot be."
>
> This same man dwelt by the road along which the King's followers had to pass. And when the Minister's elephant reached this spot, he called to him and said, "Come with us and see the God ride in his chariot!"

But the man quietly replied, "I dare not seek after God in the King's fashion."

"How should you ever have such luck again as to see the God ride in his chariot?" asked the Minister.

"Ah, when God himself comes to my door," answered the man.

At this the Minister laughed out loud, saying, "Fool! You think God will come to your door! Yet a King must travel far to see him!"

And the man answered, "Who but God visits the poor?"[1]

Indeed, who but God visits the poor? As our world bifurcates increasingly into very rich countries and very impoverished countries, it is a sad fact that rich people and poor people have fewer and fewer chances to meet one another. Yet at the same time, omnipresent media show us vivid images from one another's living rooms. The poor see the lifestyles of the rich and famous. The rich in turn know the lopsided allocation of the world's resources and see on the nightly news the fearful violence bred in slums. For the most part, the rich avoid associating with folks from "the other side of the tracks" in their own hometowns, much less in distant lands. The well-to-do may go to developing nations to extract gold or oil or timber or labor, or to snap photos of wildlife from the safety of air-conditioned safari vans, but certainly not to visit shantytowns. Certainly not to listen, really listen, to the cries of the poor. That is left to God—and to those moved by God to stand with the poor.

As the gulf widens between these two disparate worlds, the rich nations have curiously begun to feel themselves threatened by the poor of the world. I say curiously, because surely any objective analysis would yield the opposite conclusion—namely, that it is the rich who have oppressed the poor throughout history, not vice versa. To shore up their own insecurity, however, the world's most powerful nations are now passing laws and building walls to keep others out.

The privileged, meanwhile, live in gated communities. It brings to mind the parable of the rich man and Lazarus, a story that must have stupefied Jesus' listeners on first hearing because of its inversion of fortunes for rich and poor:

> There was a rich man who dressed in purple garments and fine linen and dined sumptuously each day. And lying at his door was a poor man named Lazarus, covered with sores, who would gladly have eaten his fill of the scraps that fell from the rich man's table. (Lk 16:19–21)

As the story unfolds, Lazarus dies and is lofted into glorious union with Abraham, his father in faith. The rich man also dies, but he is shunted off to everlasting torment in the fires of Gehenna.[2]

What, we might ask, did the rich man do to deserve such a miserable fate? Obviously he was well off, for only the wealthy could afford the purple dye that made his clothing so distinctive; but being rich is not a sin. The way Jesus structures the story, the rich man's fate definitely has something to do with Lazarus. The narrative, however, does not mention any actual contact between the two men. There is no indication that the rich man abused Lazarus or sent his servants out to beat him. The story doesn't even imply that he walked past him and refused to help. It simply says that the poor man "lay outside the gate." One can only conclude that the rich man never opened that gate to Lazarus, never offered him welcome or hospitality, never cared what or who lay outside the comfortable confines of his own daily routine.

Apparently, the rich man never interacted with Lazarus, and *that* is why the rich man never met God.

This parable haunts me. It forces me to ask myself: *Where are my gates, my borders? Where do I draw the line, telling myself it isn't necessary to care about anyone outside the particular orbit of my current concerns?*

The story of the rich man and Lazarus isn't really a story about helping the poor. It seems, rather, to be a wake-up call for the rich. It's not about changing the situation of the poor so much as it is about being changed ourselves, so that we become aware of our relationship with those who lie outside our gates. It's about the kind of conversion that opens our eyes so that we can no longer overlook the suffering of others.

There are, of course, many who do respond to the poor at our gates. The Western world, on the whole, has a fairly generous track record for doing the works of mercy: feeding the hungry, giving water to the thirsty, sheltering the homeless, sometimes even visiting the imprisoned. In the twenty-first century, however, that kind of almsgiving no longer suffices. Today, in addition to these works of mercy, we must be about the works of justice.

The works of justice usually make us uncomfortable, and often elicit the most strenuous protest from churchgoers who feel that religion has no rightful place in secular affairs and nothing to say about how the world should be structured. Such dismissal of work on behalf of the world's poor conveniently ignores the prophets as well as the teaching of Jesus. Any religion that limits itself to private devotion is spiritually bankrupt.

Our American ethic of rugged individualism—that spirit of pulling oneself up by one's bootstraps and overcoming adversity by diligent personal effort—feeds a subtle stance of superiority, of blaming the poor for being poor. Their poverty must be their own fault. They are lazy. They have too many children. They haven't saved wisely. They have failed to plan ahead.

Even more insidiously, all of us (rich and poor alike) seem to have been born with the stubborn karmic belief that "we get what we deserve." If God is pleased with me, I prosper. On the other hand, if my lot in life is mired in misery, I must have done something wrong to deserve such punishment. It's only fair.

Even young children view the world this way.

After escaping from Laos in 1980 by swimming across the Mekong River to Thailand with Boun, his four-year-old son, Bouapheng told me how they were picked up by the police, registered, and then escorted to Nong Khai refugee camp. As they walked toward the barbed-wire fence enclosing the camp and saw the high guard towers manned by rifle-toting soldiers, Bouapheng tried to make the best of the situation.

"This is our new home," he said to his son.

"No, it isn't," answered Boun. "This is a prison. Father, what did we do wrong?"

Pain lined Bouapheng's face as he asked me, "How can I explain to my son that we are not criminals?"

Many years after hearing Bouapheng's question, I was participating in a Catholic liturgy at one of the many churches scattered through-out Kakuma Refugee Camp in northern Kenya. About three hundred Sudanese refugees and I sat on raised mounds of dried mud fashioned as pews. We prayed and sang together in the swelteringly hot mud-brick and thatch-roofed church. Then came time for the homily. Up to the altar strode a visiting priest. He proceeded to harangue the con-gregation for thirty miserable minutes about their guilt, demanding that they scrutinize their hearts to find their sinfulness: "If you had not committed terrible sins, you would not have become refugees. God is punishing you! This is the consequence for your wrongdoings." Let-ting no one off the hook, he warned, "If you cannot recall your sin, then think harder. Examine your consciences. Find it!" And while I sat there fighting back a powerful urge to strangle that priest with my bare hands, the refugees swallowed his words whole, tears on their faces, worry further lining their already burdened brows.

When the attacks occurred in the United States on 9/11, sever-al refugees who had recently arrived to the States came to me to con-fess their secret fear that the terrorist assaults were somehow their own personal fault—that they, who had suffered from wars all their lives, had somehow dragged this punishment with them into their new homeland, like some punitive ball-and-chain they could never shake off. "What have I done?" they asked, genuinely horrified. "The war that chased me from Sudan to Ethiopia to Kenya has followed me here. Now I've put innocent Americans in danger."

In broad daylight we dismiss this kind of magical thinking, but in our own more vulnerable moments, we lapse into similar illogic. We unconsciously assume that God is made in our image, that God punishes and rewards us according to our actions. We want to be on the winning side, standing with the righteous, the ones with clean hands who are spared suffering. We believe that God's favor can only be earned by effort on our part, can only be certain when all is going well in our lives. We forget God's promise to be close to the poor and brokenhearted. We pray to a crucified Lord and yet incongruously expect that, if we try our best to be good, harm will not touch us. And if it does, we must surely deserve it.

Such thinking blocks insight into the structural causes of injustice in our world. If misfortune is believed to be a personal matter, then so is its remedy. If I see a poor man, I can donate a few coins or volunteer at the local soup kitchen. I've done my part. I sleep well at night. However, if impoverishment is recognized to be the result of forces much larger than individual choice—if it results primarily from systemic injustice—then a very different approach is required.

This approach is far more unsettling.

I have a copy of a disturbing photo, taken in southern Sudan during the long civil war: it shows a severely skeletal youth, perhaps fifteen years old, naked and crawling on hands and knees along a dirt path. All of his bones are visible beneath his too-tight skin. His head is tilted feebly upward toward a man who is walking briskly past him. The man is clothed in flowing white robes, has sandals on his feet, and is carrying a large plastic bag of rice in his hand. The rice is just beyond the reach of the child.[3]

I ask people, "What do you see in this picture?" The responses are always the same: *I see a starving child. I see a rich man ignoring the child. I see food in his hand. I see that the child is crawling; he has no dignity, whereas the rich man stands upright.*

No one ever sees—because it isn't apparent without thoughtful analysis—the structural injustice that caused this scene.

Then I ask, "What is the remedy for this suffering?" Invariably the responses are predictable: *share the rice, feed the child, clothe him, help him to stand.* These are the works of mercy—all very good and all very necessary. But no one ever mentions the works of justice.

What else has contributed to this awful scene? By asking the broader questions about what is happening here, we see a different, more complex reality. Why is this child naked and starving when there is a well-dressed man with food nearby? How did such a thing come to pass? What larger forces are at work?

A little research would tie this picture to satellite photos from two decades earlier indicating the existence of huge oil fields in southern Sudan. That revelation led the Khartoum government to arrange for oil drilling and then the construction of a pipeline to transport that southern oil into the northern government's coffers, where its profits financed a huge military build-up. That military used its newly purchased airplanes to bomb heavily along the oil pipeline corridor in order to "depopulate" the region of its troublesome southerners. Those tens-of-thousands of southerners then became refugees, fleeing the villages that had the misfortune to sit along that huge swath of land designated now only for oil workers. The refugees then walked for many months across unforgiving terrain. Thousands died along the way, and some few ended up in pictures like the one I have described.

So what do we see now in that picture? Oil. Greed. The rape of land to benefit not those who live on it, but distant powers. The unmitigated consumption of fuel for developed countries to sustain unsustainable lifestyles. The willingness of some to kill for control. The brutal displacement of innocent peoples. The intentional creation of massive refugee populations, with their consequent suffering and starvation.

From this perspective, we see the urgent need for works of justice: equitable sharing of land, moderation on the part of developed countries for nonrenewable resources, and an end to the madness of producing and selling arms. We see that the works of mercy without the works of justice can never bring lasting peace. We see that millions of people become impoverished because of global imbalances and structural sins, not because of quirks of their personality or individual failings.

The prophets of old hammered their listeners about such societal injustice. They would not have been polite dinner guests. In the Hebrew Scriptures, for example, Amos likens the wealthy who recline on ivory couches to "fat cows" who feed themselves while turning a blind eye to the plight of their neighbors. He cannot understand their self-preoccupation. You have everything you need, he says, "yet you are not made ill by the collapse of your brother Joseph?"[4]

But what would make us care about the sufferings of strangers in distant parts of the world? How can we become truly compassionate?

One of my dear friends, a former refugee from Eritrea, bears the name *Alemseged*, which means "I bow before the world." Reflecting on his name, I wonder, *how could any person attain that kind of reverence and humility?* If we all bowed low to one another, as Abraham did long ago to the three strange angels, would wars cease? If we made such remarkable reverence habitual, would compassion expand in us? If we bent the knees of our heart toward others a little more often, would caring begin to displace self-protection? I wonder.

I do believe that *mehdtah*, profound compassion, arises from the core wisdom uncovered by mystics of all the world's great religions—namely, that *we are all connected*. Like today's quantum physicists, who marvel at the intricate effects that even the tiniest particles have on the entire universe. Like ecologists, pointing out how the toxic clouds formed by pollution in China can drift across the Pacific to California in less than three weeks. Like the astronauts, able to see our earth as a fragile blue marble hurtling through space, lacking national boundaries or reasons for war. *Mehdtah* rises from that unshakable experience of original unity that cannot be shattered by superficial differences.

In the 2002 Hollywood remake of the film *The Four Feathers*, which chronicles the British army's defeat in northern Sudan by the Muslim

Mahdi forces in 1898, the life of Harry, the British leading man, is dramatically saved (more than once) by a black African man from the Nuba mountains who appears to be an escaped slave. Harry is bewildered by the stranger's kindness—heroism, really—in repeatedly rescuing him. The stranger, a Muslim named Abou, had repeatedly placed himself in extreme danger, even to the point of ending up in prison with him to engineer his escape.

Harry finally asks Abou, "Why did you save my life?"

Abou's response is utterly devoid of romanticism or friendship. He doesn't say that he felt sorry for Harry or wanted to make some grand gesture to rescue this foolhardy Brit who was so out of his element in the Sahara, or even that he was saving Harry's life to earn merit for himself. No, Abou's response is only about God.

To answer Harry's question, Abou shrugs his shoulders and says, "I had to. God put you in my way."

I had to. God put you in my way. Those two sentences concretize the imperative of *mehdtah*: Our lives have intersected, yours and mine, so I must assist you in every way possible. I must share my scarce supply of water with you when you are dying of thirst and help you escape from a prisoner-of-war camp. It's not a matter, in the end, of feelings or altruism. Not even a matter for choice. God has simply put you in my way. I cannot proceed until I have addressed your needs.

In English, the phrase *in my way* generally connotes something annoying, an obstacle, an unwanted interruption. Abou gives it a very different twist. The poor who cross my path, or of whom I become aware, have a claim on me. I must tend to them if they are in need. We are all related.

One of my favorite paintings is Gustav Klimt's *The Kiss*. Its embracing lovers shimmer in robes of gold and silver and black on a carpet strewn with flowers. The cloaks wrapping man and woman dazzle and merge, generating an image of such complete intimacy that the two figures almost disappear into each other, leaving the impression of rapture, of complete communion.

Looking at Klimt's mesmerizing art moves me in ways difficult to explain. For me it hints at God's permanent posture toward each of us and all of creation. *The Kiss* reminds me that we are all swept up in God's passionate embrace. This is God's permanent posture toward us. We are all drawn together and made uniquely lovely by the cloak of God's presence. It's like an unending wedding procession. We are all on the way to God's tent, which is open on all four sides. Each person, each tree, each clod of dirt or wisp of cloud, each bird and bear, each lamb and lion, each friend and enemy—one by one, each disappearing into the folds of God's warm welcome for a long moment and then emerging fresh and beautiful to behold.

Some of us get in line over and over again, unable to contain our joy. Others seem not to know what awaits them or even that they are in line or how they are already being transformed in the waiting. No matter. We are all in this together. We are all kin.

If this is true, why are we not overcome by such unspeakable tenderness? Why are we not, in turn, approaching one another with awe? Grace—those leading strings of love connecting us all—permeates all of creation. Nothing is left outside this holiness. God is always flowing toward us.

God is in our experience of the wake flame within us that can never be quenched. In the reckless surrendering of our hearts to strangers. In our decisions to make some space for the unexpected and to tend, despite all inconvenience, whatever is put "in our way."

Those who have met this God find that their circle of concern continually widens. "The truest impulse toward work for social justice," writes Belden Lane in *The Solace of Fierce Landscapes*, "grows not out of an anxious sense of pity for others or a grandly noble desire to serve, but out of the abandonment of the self in God."[5] Through such encounters God does transform us, saints and sinners alike.

Dorothee Soelle describes every spiritual journey as a lifelong movement from amazement, to letting go, to resistance.[6] First, there is always amazement: being stunned by joy, filled with gratitude, captivated by beauty and goodness and grace and love. Then come times of failure, loss and darkness, times of wrestling with unbelief; dyings, great and small; chances to face the fierceness of a Love beyond grasping. Finally, great gentleness emerges in our hearts—*mehdtah*, an expansive compassion for *all* that exists. Gentle, yes, but equally bold, it stands resolutely against whatever is not loving, resisting all that is not yet aligned with justice and mercy, no matter how impossible the odds.

This, then, may be the world's only hope for peace: that all of us, friends and enemies, allies and foes, brothers and sisters and strangers alike, understand we meet as guests together in "God's own tent." That, like the prophets, we allow ourselves to be made ill by the collapse of our brother Joseph, and we commit ourselves to changing the unjust structures that caused that collapse. That we, like Alem, learn to bow before the world. That we, like God, choose to visit the poor. That we who have abundant resources begin to share freely with everyone else in line. That our fear of strangers gives way to the risk of welcoming them.

Each step in that direction moves our bruised and broken world closer to the day when mercy and justice shall kiss.

$\mathscr{A}$CKNOWLEDGMENTS

This book owes much to the Sisters of Mercy, whose lives of compassion have shaped and supported my own, and who granted me sabbatical time in which to write; to Reza Odabaee, the co-worker extraordinaire who introduced me to the Persian poet Rumi; and to all my colleagues in refugee work worldwide, whose daily dedication to the world's displaced goes largely unheralded.

I offer apologies for any reflections in this book that originated elsewhere. The cumulative wisdom of others has surely seeped into my bones over the years, taken on my shape and size, blended with my own thoughts, and emerged in this writing. Where I am conscious of another source, I have given attribution. For the rest, all I can say is that I honor those who have taught me along the way.

Most of all, however, I bow to the refugees whose lives have blessed my own these past twenty-five years—survivors, all of them, from war, upheaval, and persecution in Afghanistan, Algeria, Angola, Bangladesh, Bosnia-Herzegovina, Burma/Myanmar, Burundi, Cambodia, Cameroon, China, Colombia, Congo/Brazzaville, Congo/Kinshasa, Croatia, Cuba, El Salvador, Eritrea, Ethiopia, Guatemala, Haiti, Honduras, Iran, Iraq, Ivory Coast, Kenya, Kosovo, Laos, Liberia, Mozambique, Nepal,

Nicaragua, Nigeria, Peru, Poland, Russia, Rwanda, Serbia, Sierra Leone, Somalia, Sri Lanka, Sudan, The Philippines, Tibet, Togo, and Vietnam.

Their voices deserve listeners. Their lives testify to the gracious God who loves us all but stands closest to the poor.

*N*OTES

PREFACE

1. Mechtild of Magdeburg, "Of all that God has shown me," ed. Jane Hirshfield, in *Women in Praise of the Sacred* (New York: HarperCollins, 1994), 96.

A NEW WAY OF LOVING

1. Adapted from *Teaching Your Children about God*, by David J. Wolpe; quoted in *Spiritual Literacy*, by Frederick and Mary Ann Brussat (New York: Simon and Schuster, 1996), 128.

2. The volunteer, whose finger had to be amputated, declined to press charges against Nhia Bee.

3. Voltaire, *Candide and Other Writings*, ed. Haskell M. Block (New York: Random House, 1984), 371–2.

GOD WHO WEEPS

1. Adapted from a paraphrase of Chesterton's story in *Everlasting Man* by Ronald Rolheiser in his book, *Holy Longing: The Search for a Christian Spirituality* (New York: Doubleday, 1999), 89.

2. As Richard Rohr writes, "Remember that the opposite of love is not hatred but control. God remains in love. . . . That is the beauty and the limitation of those who love. They can give up control, and they can weep instead of explain." *Job and the Mystery of Suffering* (New York: The Crossroad Publishing Company, 1996), 60.

3. C.S. Lewis, *The Four Loves* (New York, Harcourt, Brace & Co, 1991), 121.

A Knock on the Door

1. Cited on "Your Daily Dig," www.Bruderhof.com, October 10, 2005.

2. Ibid.

Food You Know Not Of

1. In the month of January, northeastern Thailand hosts its annual Banana Festival, during which the loveliest of the village girls compete for the title of Miss Banana. Alas, unlike Marilyn Monroe, who was once crowned Miss California Artichoke in her pre-Hollywood days, I was not chosen to be the Banana Queen.

2. The Hollywood scriptwriters may have been influenced by the ancient Greeks. According to Geoffrey Abbott's book, *Execution: The Guillotine, the Pendulum, the Thousand Cuts, the Spanish Donkey, and 66 Other Ways of Putting Someone to Death*, they utilized the "cyphon method" of killing, which involved securing their naked victim under a hot sun and smearing him with milk and honey, then leaving him to the stinging insects.

COME AND SEE

1. After much public pressure by advocacy groups in the United States, Chevron withdrew from its interests in Sudan. It was quickly replaced by China.

2. When I returned to California, the *San Jose Mercury News* printed a full-page Op Ed piece that I wrote to honor her memory and published the photo I had taken of Angela and her child.

3. *Time* magazine, April 5, 1993: 16.

GOD DOES NOT KILL

1. For a compelling first-person account from a child soldier, cf. *A Long Way Gone: Memoirs of a Boy Soldier* (New York: Farrar, Straus & Giroux, 2007).

2. Jeffrey Gettleman summarizes the shift to child soldiers in "The Perfect Weapon for the Meanest Wars," *The New York Times*, April 29, 2007, Week in Review, 1.

3. George W. Cornell, "Widespread Tortures Parallel Abuse of Christ," *The Gettysburg Times* (April 15, 1981), 5.

4. Excerpted from the poem "The Weighing," *The October Palace: Poems by Jane Hirshfield* (New York: Harper Perennial, 1994), 79.

CREATURE DISCOMFORT

1. A similar story, with photo, captured global headlines in August 2007. A two-hundred-foot-long spider web, apparently the work of millions of Guatemalan long-jawed spiders working together, appeared in a Texas park, encasing a large cluster of oak trees.

2. Mark Moffett, "Big Bite: Little Known and Lightning Fast, Wind Scorpions Wield the Desert's Most Powerful Jaws," *National Geographic* magazine, July 2004.

3. Sadly, a Catholic nun did die from a camel spider bite in Kakuma during the summer of 2007.

THIS FLOWING TOWARD ME

1. See, for example, Isaiah 43:4 and 49:15; Hosea 11; Jeremiah 33:40; Zephaniah 3:17–18.

2. "You, Neighbor God," by Rainer Maria Rilke, *Poems from the Book of Hours* (New York: New Directions Publishing Corporation, 1941),13.

3. John Moyne and Coleman Barks, *Open Secret: Versions of Rumi* (Boston: Shambhala Publications, 1999), 74.

4. This constant "towardness" of God's loving Presence is, I suppose, what theologians call "grace." Grace, however, carries the unfortunate connotation of being some sort of "thing" to be earned or forfeited, stored up or lost. I prefer Rumi's active sense of movement, of a relationship growing, of God leaning toward us lovingly.

5. Jack Kornfield, *After the Ecstasy, the Laundry: How the Heart Grows Wise on the Spiritual Path* (New York: Bantam Books, 2000).

6. Robert Francis, *Robert Francis: Collected Poems 1936–1976* (Boston: University of Massachusetts Press, 1985), 149.

7. *Evelyn Underhill: Modern Guide to the Ancient Quest for the Holy*, ed. Dana Greene (New York: SUNY Press, 1988), 75.

8. *Etty Hillesum, An Interrupted Life*, trans. Arnold J. Pomerans (New York: Henry Holt & Co., 1996).

9. Ibid.

10. Ibid.

11. "The Opening of Eyes," by David Whyte, *Songs for Coming Home: Poems* (Langley, WA: Many Rivers Company, 1989).

12. Stephen Mitchell, "Baal Shem Tov," *Parables and Portraits* (New York: Harper Perennial, 1994), 35.

13. Brother David Steindl-Rast is eloquent on the unbreakable connection between gratefulness and joy. Cf. *Gratefulness, the Heart of Prayer: An Approach to Life in Fullness* (Ramsey, NJ: Paulist Press, 1984).

14. A phrase from *The Little Prince*, written by famed French aviator Antoine de Saint-Exupéry.

15. May Sarton, *Journal of a Solitude* (New York: W.W. Norton and Company, 1992), 99.

16. Andrew Harvey, *Perfume of the Desert* (Wheaton, IL: Quest Books, 1999), 33.

STRANGER GOD

1. Henri Nouwen, *Reaching Out* (New York: Image Books, 1975), 68.

2. The commandment to welcome the stranger is second in frequency only to the great commandment to love God with all one's heart and mind and strength and soul.

3. This theme appears in other major faith traditions as well. The Hindu scripture Taitiriya Upanishad tells us: "The guest is a representative of God" (1.11.2). Likewise, the Qur'an reminds us to "serve God . . . and do good to . . . orphans, those in need, neighbors who are near, neighbors who are strangers, the companion by your side, the wayfarer that you meet, and those who have nothing" (4:36).

4. "Song of a Man Who Has Come Through," *D.H. Lawrence, Complete Poems*, ed. Vivian de Sola Pinto and Warren F. Roberts (New York: Penguin Classics, 1994), 250.

5. *St. John of the Cross, The Spiritual Canticle and Poems*, ed. E. Alison Peers, (New York: Continuum, 1999), 219.

6. "Vacillation," from *The Collected Poems of Y. B.Yeats*, ed. Richard J. Finneran (New York: Scribner, 1996), 249–250.

7. An excerpt from a Haiku by the Japanese poet Issa.

8. Celebrated during April in Laos and Thailand.

9. *Reaching Out*, 71.

10. Homer, *The Odyssey,* trans. Allen Mandelbaum (Berkeley: University of California Press, 1990), 17.485–7.

11. The parable was Jesus' response to a lawyer's question, "What must I do to have eternal life?"

12. Thomas Merton, *Raids on the Unspeakable* (New York: New Directions Publishing, 1966), 72.

13. Apology 15 in *The Anti-Nicene Fathers*, as quoted in *Charities USA* magazine, first qtr. 1994.

14. From a talk given by William Spohn.

15. Annie Dillard, *Teaching a Stone to Talk* (New York: Harper Perennial, 1988), 52.

16. This evocative phrase is from Angela Hartigan, a Sister of Mercy working in the slums of Nairobi, in her Op Ed article, "Being Poor in Kenya Means a Life of Insults," *Sunday Nation*, Nairobi, July 15, 2007.

17. "God's Grandeur," *Poems of Gerald Manley Hopkins*, ed. Robert Bridges (Whitefish, MT: Kessinger Publications, 2004), 19–20.

18. The phrase is from St. Paul's letter to the Ephesians (Eph 2:14).

MERCY AND JUSTICE SHALL KISS

1. Rabindranath Tagore, *The Fugitive* (London: Macmillan, 1921).

2. Interestingly, Jesus gives a name only to the poor man in this parable. The rich man remains anonymous and, therefore, less important in the story. It's a subtle clue to divine inversion of societal values. The popular notion of Hell as a place of unquenchable fire probably originated from Jesus' imagery of the condemned being banished to the "fires of Gehenna." Gehenna was the main garbage dump outside Jerusalem, a place where fires burned day and night. Jesus' imagery highlights not the flames, but the social isolation of the place, its existence outside the realm of human community.

3. The photo, by James Nachtwey, appeared in *US News & World Report*, Sep 14, 1998. The caption reads: "A well-nourished man steals grain from a starving child at U.N. feeding center in Ajiep in southern Sudan."

4. Amos 6:6. Here the term "Joseph" refers not to a person but to an entire tribe.

5. Belden Lane, *The Solace of Fierce Landscapes* (New York: Oxford University Press, 1998), 76.

6. Dorthee Soelle, *The Silent Cry: Mysticism and Resistance* (Minneapolis: Fortress Press, 2001), 88ff.

Marilyn Lacey, R.S.M., has worked with refugees for the past twenty-five years, both in displaced persons camps in Africa and Asia, and as Director of Refugee Services with Catholic Charities in San Jose, California. In 2001 she was honored by the Dalai Lama as an "Unsung Hero of Compassion" and has long been an advocate for refugees and migrants. She holds an MA in social work from UC Berkeley, and in 2008 founded the non-profit Mercy Beyond Borders, whose mission is to partner with displaced women and children overseas in ways that help them move out of extreme poverty.

Books That Inspire

Mother Teresa's Prescription
Finding Happiness and Peace in Service
Paul A. Wright, MD

The inspiring story of a successful doctor's transformation after he seeks counsel from Mother Teresa and embraces a life of service and compassion.

◆ ◆ ◆

"This book presents many of Mother Teresa's own great spiritual ideas and ideals and inspires other people to go on doing the work she did so well on earth."
Theodore M. Hesburgh, C.S.C.
President Emeritus, University of Notre Dame

ISBN: 9781594710728 / 128 pages / $9.95

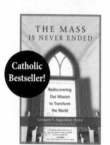

The Mass Is Never Ended
Rediscovering Our Mission to Transform the World
Gregory F. Augustine Pierce

Noted author Gregory F. Augustine Pierce examines the Mass through the lens of the dismissal rite, reinvigorating Catholics' understanding of the Mass.

◆ ◆ ◆

"When you begin to realize that you are called to mission, and how the Mass can be celebrated from the perspective of the dismissal—for mission!—your outlook on life will be changed."

Stephen Bevans, S.V.D.
Catholic Theological Union, Chicago

ISBN: 9781594710698 / 128 pages / $10.95

This War Is the Passion
Caryll Houselander

Originally published in 1941, this book by the renowned British mystic and spiritual writer Caryll Houselander is once again new as modern readers learn from Houselander's encouragement of her compatriots to view their experience of World War II through the lens of Christ's passion.
ISBN: 9780870612459 / 192 pages / $11.95

Practicing Peace
A Devotional Walk through the Quaker Tradition
Catherine Whitmire

"Cathy Whitmire has drawn on her own experience and on the rich heritage of Quaker peacemaking to craft an absorbing book, one which will inspire and guide people of any faith and of none."

Harvey Cox
Harvard Divinity School

ISBN: 9781933495071 / 272 pages / $16.95